GETTING
LEAN

An Introduction to Lean Business
Practices in the Form of an
Entertaining Novel

GETTING LEAN

An Introduction to Lean Business
Practices in the Form of an
Entertaining Novel

---

*Making Companies Globally Competitive
Series*

Jerry Feingold

WCM Associates
Fort Wayne, Indiana
www.wcmfg.com

Getting Lean

By
Jerry Feingold

Copyright 2005 by WCM Associates.
All rights reserved.
Printed in the United States of America

WCM Associates
P.O. Box 8035
Fort Wayne, IN   46898-8035
260-637-8064
www.wcmfg.com

ISBN # 0-9662906-8-2

Front and rear cover design by:
Robert Howard Graphic Design
rhoward@bookgraphics.com

Book and text design by WCM Associates

Printed and bound by:
Thomson-Shore, Inc.
Dexter, MI
(734)426-3939

Library of Congress Catalog Card Number: 2004115710

I gratefully dedicate this book to Ruthann, my wonderful wife.

CONTENTS

Contents

INTRODUCTION

American Business is in the midst of a revolution. In 1947, according to the Federal Reserve of Chicago, 35% of America's workforce was employed in manufacturing. By 2002, employment in U.S. manufacturing had fallen to 12%—two-thirds less than 55 years ago! If you look at the goods sold in your local store, it looks as if everything was manufactured and imported from a foreign country. American manufacturers are fleeing our shores in pursuit of cheap labor. Manufacturing's future in America is in jeopardy!

Despite cheap labor elsewhere, there are many reasons to keep manufacturing at home. American factories employ fewer workers than their low-wage foreign counterparts—one reason that demonstrates that labor costs no longer make or break the decision about where to put a factory. Payroll costs in America account for only 11% of overall manufacturing costs; meanwhile, growing demand for prompt and speedy delivery is much more important today than are relative wages, and is another reason to keep producing at home.

Also, many companies often underestimate the cost of overseas manufacturing, particularly those associated with transportation, extra inventory, and political security risks.

Lean manufacturing techniques in America, however, have allowed those companies that employ them to enjoy soaring manufacturing productivity. Since 1970, America's manufacturing output has more than doubled. American manufacturing output is almost 50% higher today than in 1992 thanks in large measure to Lean approaches in manufacturing.

This is a Lean handbook. Although it reads like a novel, *Getting Lean* is intended to be a guide or manual with specific tools necessary in analyzing a factory in order to discover its sources of waste and opportunities for improvement.

Getting Lean describes in detail how to implement improvements very quickly. The improvements include one-piece flow, a simple Kanban system, rapid changeover, Total Productive Maintenance and 5S industrial housekeeping,

Woven throughout the book is the author's philosophy of industrial management which, while heavily focused on creating a highly competitive organization, is based upon such concepts as:

- ◆ The necessity of embracing change

- ◆ The value of a success plan

- ◆ Learning and profiting from mistakes

- ◆ Elimination of fear in the workplace

- ◆ The need to manage for total system efficiency rather than local efficiency

- ◆ Engaging the hearts and minds of the entire workforce

This book is written in the form of a novel. The story is true. It is a compilation of real-life experiences about transforming troubled factories into LEAN enterprises. The names of people, places, and products have been changed to protect the innocent as well as the guilty.

To make the book more of a useful textbook and less of a story, each chapter ends with a discussion called, "From a LEAN management standpoint: What's going on in this chapter?"

GLOSSARY OF TERMS

Cells—The layout of assembly operators or of a cluster of machines performing sequential operations in a one-piece-flow manner.

Changeover—The process of changing a device to perform a new operation. This could involve such activities as changing cutting tools, changing color of paint or changing the assembly fixtures on a manual assembly line.

Cycle Time—*Actual* time an operator takes to complete their operation. This is contrasted to takt time which is the *theoretical* time required.

Five S (5S)—This is a standardized method of industrial housekeeping. It gets its name from the five Japanese terms beginning with the letter S. These five terms are: *Seiri (Sort)*, which means to identify items that are no longer needed in the area. The Red Tag campaign accomplishes that. *Seiton (Straighten)*, means to arrange and identify the remaining materials in an orderly manner. *Seiso (Sweep)*, means to scrub everything clean. *Seiketso (Schedule)*, means to frequently engage in the above three disciplines. *Shitsuke (Sustain)*, means to build self-discipline so that 5S becomes standardized.

Flow—The progression of a product along the value stream with no stoppages or rework.

Just-in-Time—The JIT production system originated at the Toyota Motor Company by Taiichi Ohno. Simply stated, it is a method of delivering the right quantity of the right part at the right time.

Kaikaku (Kaizen Events and Kaizen Blitzes)—Dramatic improvement in a production operation in a very short period of time by discovering and eliminating waste. It is also known as Kaizen Events or Kaizen Blitzes.

Kaizen—Literally translated as *continuous improvement*.

Kanban—Japanese word meaning *signal*. It typically is a card attached to a bin of parts. The card is used to signal upstream production processes that a replenishment point has been reached and that a certain number of parts must now be delivered to a designated location.

Lead Time—The time the customer has to wait for the product after placing an order.

MRP—Material Requirements Planning. A computer system used to determine materials usage and timing.

MRP II—Manufacturing Resource Planning. An expansion of MRP, which includes capacity planning and simulations to review alternate production plans.

MUDA—Waste. There are seven classes of Muda. Muda of overproduction (making more than needed or sooner than needed), Muda of inventory (more than the minimum required), Muda of making rejects or doing rework, Muda of motion (unnecessary bending, reaching or straining), Muda of processing (avoidable unnecessary work such as deburring or cleaning), Muda of waiting and Muda of conveyance (transportation of materials between operations).

Process—A series of steps required to create an end result. Each process has an input and an output. The process could produce a design, an answer to a customer, a step along an assembley line or a complete product.

Pull—The movement of a product from downstream to upstream. The pull is created by customer demand rather than from a central scheduling point.

Sensei—A master or teacher.

SMED—Single Minute Exchange of Dies. A discipline developed by Toyota to radically reduce the changeover time of presses. The system was originally deployed to reduce the time to change a die in a press from twelve hours to less than ten minutes.

Spaghetti Diagram—Also called a *dance chart*. A sketch showing the path a part takes through its steps of production. It is called a spaghetti diagram because it looks like a plate of spaghetti.

Takt Time—The rate of production that matches the actual rate of sales. It is calculated by dividing the available time in a day by the daily customer demand.

TPM—Total Productive Maintenance. A discipline developed by Toyota to assure the availability of machines so that production isn't interrupted. TPM is used to minimize unexpected breakdowns or slowdowns of machinery.

Value Stream—The activities required to provide a customer with a final product. The activities begin with product conception and ends with the delivery of the product to the end customer.

Value Stream Map—A graphic depiction of the value stream. The map is a sketch that shows such details as cycle times, inventory levels and communication routes.

CHAPTER 1

WHAT HAVE I DONE?

It seemed like yesterday that Larry Smith got the call from the management recruiter. Actually, it was three months ago. Larry wasn't looking for a job when the recruiter called. The closest he had come to thinking about a job change was his recurrent illusory daydream about chucking everything and moving to Vermont to make wooden toys.

Larry had been working for Superior Aerospace Controls for eight years. He had worked his way up to production manager of the fabrication and assembly department. He liked his job, liked his boss, and was at the point where the job had become almost routine. The only nagging fears he had were about the outlook for aerospace contractors as a result of defense spending cutbacks and the pressure the aircraft manufacturers were putting on their parts suppliers. Those thoughts usually led to his daydream about making wooden toys.

The recruiter told him about the opportunity—a manufacturing director's job 150 miles away at Sonic Labs, a company that made loudspeakers. Not only was the salary fantastic, there was a $10,000 sign-on bonus. Once Larry agreed to visit them for that first interview, he felt as though he had stepped onto a train going 300 miles an hour that he could not step off of.

The three months flew by for Larry and Sue. They had to sell their house and buy a new one in Fair Lawn. They moved from their 950-square- foot ranch style house built in 1978 to a 2300- square-foot center hall colonial in the brand new Royal Hills development situated in an apple orchard on the outskirts of Fair Lawn—a twenty-five minute drive to Sonic Labs for Larry.

Emotions were running on overdrive. Sue was excited about her new house and the prospect of being able to use some of the $10,000 sign-on bonus to furnish it. She was also sick with guilt about leaving her parents who lived less than ten minutes away from their old house. They had two children. Tommy was eight and Hannah was four. Sue's dad had become very close to Hannah. Sue was very close to her parents, especially her mom. People often mistook them for sisters. Larry hadn't been sleeping well, especially after his first day at Sonic.

The string of interviews three months ago went fine. Initially, he met with the recruiter who de-scribed Sonic as a highly profitable company whose biggest problem was simply to cope with their rapid growth. Sonic loudspeakers had become a fad product, especially among college kids. Sonics played loud, had lots of bass, and weren't expen-sive. The recruiter presented Larry and three other candidates to Sonic and Larry won. Larry's inter-views at Sonic were fun for him. Although he wasn't one hundred percent convinced that he wanted to change jobs, he did get a new suit for the interview and got his hair cut.

His first interview was with Ken Baley the personnel director. Ken seemed preoccupied during the interview and spent no more than ten minutes with Larry discussing the company's growth and the problem he was having hiring factory as well as staff personnel. Ken dismissed Larry after asking him the routine questions that Larry thought must be listed in a book for personnel directors on "how to conduct an assessment interview." Ken then had his secretary take Larry to a conference room to be interviewed by a team of five people who would become Larry's peers if he were given the job. These guys were great. They seemed to be having a good time and were very enthusiastic about Sonic and were supportive of one another. These men were running the materials organization, engineering, and finance. Their biggest problems were those associated with growth. The position Larry was applying for—Manufacturing Director—was vacant because the incumbent had "left." Whatever that meant. The team was mostly interested in Larry's accomplishments at Superior with the implementation of a material control system.

He thought he did well with that interview because the team passed him onto the VP of Operations, Jim Brady. Mr. Brady must have had some military in his background. He appeared humorless, rigid, and seemed to enjoy playing the role of Mr. Tough Guy. Jim explained that he had been very busy since the past Manufacturing Director had "left" and was anxious to fill the position but was interested in finding the best candidate and would not compromise. He said he needed someone who was "results orientated," someone whom he could depend upon to run the factory; he would be willing to wait for the right candidate to come along, "irregardless" of how long it took. Larry wondered if "orientated" and "irregardless" were real words. Brady spent more time talking about himself than in asking Larry questions.

Larry was offered the job. The recruiter called him at home one evening after the interviews and breathlessly announced that Larry had the job. The recruiter couldn't believe that Larry needed a day to think it over. "What's there to think about?" asked the recruiter. Although the job was a promotion, the money great, the company growing. . .there was Jim Brady. "Do I want that guy for a boss?"

Larry took the job and lived in a hotel in Fair Lawn for six weeks, coming home on Friday nights. Sue remained at the old house while their new house was being completed and capably took care of the details of selling and moving. Those were a tough six weeks for Larry. He was isolated from the most important things in his life.

He had never been away from Sue for so long and he missed her. They had been high school sweethearts and considered each other best friends in addition to husband and wife. Sue still turned Larry on and people were always noticing that they still acted like newlyweds, even though they had been married for twelve years. They always seemed to be touching each other. Larry was very close to

Tommy, his eight year old. Tommy was a Cub Scout and Larry took an active role with the scout troop. He was on the committee and had just started to organize this year's pinewood derby, an event in which the scouts and their dads make six-inch long racecars that compete in rolling down an inclined ramp. He loved his neighborhood and considered his next-door neighbor, Bob Chase, to be his best friend. In the eight years that they had been neighbors, they had developed dozens of common interests. Most of the interests took on various forms of competition. When they fished together it became a contest for the first fish, the biggest fish, the most fish. They played tennis with competitive passion and kept a record of their games. Larry's latest contest with Bob was with tomato plants. They were competing to see who could grow the largest tomato.

Before the chain of events with the job change, Larry had bought an automatic garage door opener that he was looking forward to installing. Now he had to install it for the new owner and would probably never get the pleasure of using it.

Larry did not enjoy his evenings those six weeks away from home. He missed his family, his friends, and his house. In addition to having lonely evenings, he had serious doubts about what he had gotten himself into.

Larry's first day at work ended with asking himself, "What have I done?"

Getting signed up in the personnel department took no more than twenty minutes, after which

Larry was ushered into Jim Brady's office. The five guys who had interviewed him were there, sitting around the conference table that intersected Brady's desk at right angles. Jim was at the blackboard writing when Larry was ushered in. "Well look who's here—it's Larry Smith. You're just in time for our planning session."

This was the first time Larry had been in Jim Brady's office. His interview had been conducted in a conference room. Larry looked around the office whose walls were covered with charts. There must have been sixty charts. One section of wall was devoted to a six-foot-long sign that read:

"We want to become the premier manufacturer of loudspeakers."

Jim Brady was at the blackboard creating a list of objectives with the categories: *productivity, efficiency, machine utilization, labor utilization, on-time delivery, first pass yield.* He was creating what he called "strive objectives." He explained that he had already committed his objective in these areas to his boss Ed Turner, Sonic's President—but he wanted to create a more aggressive set of objectives that his team would "strive" to achieve. There was a hint of menace in Brady's conducting of this collaborative exercise. Larry got the impression that there would be hell to pay if the strive goals weren't hit.

It looked to Larry that Jim Brady viewed his role as one that coerces his people to commit to aggressive targets and then his main job becomes *keeping score.* Larry had never seen so many measurement charts of a factory. This guy must love scorekeeping.

Larry left his first day of work feeling sick. It was as if Jim Brady's motto should be "I don't care how you do it, just give me the results—or else." And the sign on his wall about becoming the premier manufacturer of loudspeakers— what was that supposed to be? At Superior their President, Don Esters, hated what he called "vacuous and simplistic mission and vision statements." Esters thought that many of the ones that he saw made management an object of ridicule after the employees read them. He viewed them as having no real value and containing messages that wear off quickly.

Larry spent the afternoon getting acquainted with his factory and his staff. What a mess. It looked more like a warehouse than a factory. It was as if a wind had come through and knocked everything over. Parts and tools were strewn everywhere and forklift trucks were racing through the aisles.

"Can I fix this mess?" "Does Jim Brady know what he's doing?" "Will Sonic be able to expand to satisfy their customers or will they collapse?" "Can I go back to my old job at Superior?"

Discussion—From a LEAN management standpoint: What's going on in this chapter?

Our hero has realized that his new boss might not be a very good leader. Jim Brady has a menacing tone. In W. Edward Deming's book, *Out of the Crisis*, he lists fourteen points for management to transform a company. His eighth point is: "Drive out fear so that everyone may work effectively for the company."

Creation of a non-judgmental, fear-free environment allows the workforce to be fully engaged. Otherwise an atmosphere of risk aversion could be created.

The other peculiarity about Jim Brady's method is his fascination with all those metrics.

A company doesn't need dozens of key metrics. The dashboard of an automobile serves as a good example to illustrate this point. A typical dashboard today has six instruments: fuel level, water temperature, oil pressure, battery charge, speedometer, and odometer.

If no limits were placed on the number of instruments to put onto the dashboard, dozens could fit. Things like exhaust temperature, manifold pressure, and air-fuel mixture could be monitored. But those things aren't necessary for the driver to know. Over the years, it has been established that the driver needs only those six.

The same is true in some companies. They

often create too many metrics to monitor. This not only creates a dilution of effort, it leads to useless exercises. Many metrics such as productivity, efficiency, and machine utilization are either lagging indicators or are overly aggregated.

To find out at the end of the month that productivity fell is giving a message that is too late. Abstractions such as *low efficiency* are confusing because the calculation to derive the efficiency metric is typically made up of so many elements that it is impossible to track down any root causes.

The lean production system is one in which more and more gets done with less and less.

Lean companies have learned that the effort to produce a product can be reduced by 75%; the time elapsed from order receipt to delivery of product can be reduced by 90%; and inventories can be cut by 90%. Development of meaningful metrics to achieve these lean improvements is vital.

Without these metrics, senior management often find themselves very uncomfortable on the factory floor. At one point, MBWA (management by walking around) was hailed as the latest panacea for leaders. These proved to be an ineffective tool because managers had no idea what questions to ask and were so intimidated by the factory environment that they didn't pause long enough at one spot to get the right answers.

In Lean companies, the metrics are clear to personnel at every level and are typically conspicuously posted throughout the enterprise. In Lean companies, managers go to the factory floor when there are problems. In typical companies, in time of factory problems, managers go to the conference room to plead, "It's not my fault."

Let's return to Larry's world.

CHAPTER 2

LUCKY FELLA

The Royal Hills development consisted of one hundred eighty homes divided into five phases. There were thirty homes in the Smith's phase and they were all completed within two weeks of one another. Most of the people moving in seemed to be about the same age as the Smiths. Lots of young children. They had met some of the neighbors during the two-week period when the people moved into their phase. The family across the street was named Simms. Bob Simms had moved into Royal Hills to take a job as manufacturing director for Apache Corporation. Apache made bicycle parts in a factory near Fair Lawn. The Smiths took an instant liking to the Simmses. They were about the same age and their children were about the same age. He was recruited to run Manufacturing at Apache. Apache was experiencing tremendous growth because of the new enthusiasm for cycling in America.

The houses in Royal Hills consisted of twelve different models ranging in size from 2200 to 3800 square feet. The Simms's house was the 3800 square-foot model. The Smiths had a GMC sports utility vehicle that Larry drove to work. Sue drove the "family car," a 1994 Buick Century. Simms drove a black 500 series BMW not more than six months old. His wife, Lesley, drove a brand new Volvo Station wagon. "The bicycle industry must pay a hell of a lot more than the loudspeaker industry," thought Larry.

Larry usually left for work at 6:00 AM so that he could meet with third shift before they left for the day. He typically worked until 6:30 PM so that he could spend some time with the second shift. Larry rolled into Royal Hills at about 7:00 PM every night. Sue would make the kids wait for Larry to come home before serving dinner. The family dinner was sacred to Sue and something that Larry appreciated.

Larry's morning schedule was, in a funny way, coordinated with Bob Simms's. Almost every day when Larry pulled out of his driveway, he would see Bob Simms, wearing a robe and slippers, walking down his driveway across the street to get the morning newspaper. On many evenings when Larry was coming from work and pulling into his driveway, he would see Bob Simms, wearing tennis clothes, pulling into his driveway. Obviously the guy had already come home from work and had time to play tennis. So the bicycle industry must not only pay well, it must not demand very long hours of its manufacturing executives.

CHAPTER 3

IT HITS THE FAN

It was 6:30 on a Wednesday evening. Larry was meeting with Benny DeVito, his first-shift manager and Wally Hinderer, the second-shift manager. They were in Larry's office, reviewing the production output for the day and making plans for the next day when Jim Brady walked into the office. He looked at Larry and said, "I've been working all afternoon on the month-end numbers and I'll tell you right now, they don't look too good. I'll probably be here until midnight preparing for the morning's month-end staff review."

This was going to be Larry's first month-end review. He'd been at Sonic for four weeks and until now there hadn't been one discussion with Brady about any of the charts that he kept on his office wall. Benny and Wally had warned Larry that his predecessor, Ed Boyd, dreaded those month-end meetings.

Larry didn't sleep well that night. Actually he hadn't slept well since coming to Sonic. This was the first time in his life he had experienced any sleep problems. But this was the first time in his life that he felt so insecure. College wasn't particularly challenging. Even though the engineering curriculum was difficult, there was plenty of time left over for the fraternity. Then the job at Superior wasn't particularly difficult. They had only one competitor, but not much of a competitor, so Superior had no compelling reason to improve anything.

He pulled out of his driveway at 6:30 AM. There were no lights on in the Simms house. They were still asleep.

Jim Brady's month-end staff review started at 8:00 AM. His six direct reports including Larry were assembled in his office. Jim looked angry. His face was red as he began to speak. "I've been working at this company for nine months and this is the first month we have lost money. We lost $150,000 in one month. That means we are losing money at the rate of $1.8 million per year. The losses are all in the factory. I'm not saying that the factory was doing fine until Larry Smith got here last month, but the numbers you're about to see don't paint a pretty picture of Larry's performance."

Larry couldn't believe what he was hearing. Can this guy seriously believe that he was somehow to blame for all the company's problems after only being there a few weeks? Larry's impulse was to protest or defend himself but he had not yet seen the charts Brady was talking about. Larry's first month wasn't easy. The company was growing so quickly that the only way they could get staff quickly enough was to hire temporary workers from a local agency. Forty-five percent of the labor forces were temps. "How much care would these people take in assembling the product if they feel no sense of loyalty to Sonic?" Larry would ask himself. In addition to a high defect rate (25% of everything they made had to be re-worked) his biggest problem was part shortages. The combination of the high rate of rework and the constant shortages of parts made Larry feel that his job was impossible.

Jim presented his charts. Labor efficiency was 27%. Labor productivity was 34%. "What the hell does efficiency and productivity mean? Why is one different from the other?" Larry asked himself.

$30,000 was lost on scrapped materials. On-time delivery dropped from 63% the prior month to 29% this month.

It occurred to Larry that although there were lots of charts, none of them allowed him to pinpoint root causes. As a matter of fact, he didn't see where any of the charts were useful for management decision-making.

Brady announced, "At this rate, gentlemen, none of us will have jobs three months from now and, believe me, I'm not planning on going down by myself; I'll get all of you before that happens. If you don't believe me, ask your old friend Ed Boyd— he didn't take me too seriously."

"I submitted my performance goals to my boss, Ed Turner. Achieving those goals would have meant that Sonic would show a profit of $3 million. Four weeks ago we agreed to the strive goals that would have resulted in a profit of $3.9 million. In just four weeks since, we have gone from a growing company destined to make a $3 million profit to one that will lose nearly $2 million. That's a $5 million swing. I'm not going to stand for this. I'll give you 24 hours to come up with a 'get well' plan and if I don't like the plan I'll get rid of every one of you."

Jim dismissed his staff and returned to his calculations. The staff walked together into Ellen Kane's office down the hall from Brady's. "That son of a bitch," said Ellen Kane, the director of materials. "We have a month-long problem and two weeks after the end of the month Jim-the-score-keeper announces that something went terribly wrong six weeks ago? None of us have any visibility about our financial performance until the end of the month and by that time it's too late to do anything about it. Does he view his job as pressuring us into accepting goals and then threatening us if we fail? I've been here for two years and, since Jim came here nine months ago, all I hear from him is slogans, coercion, and threats. I have very little respect for this guy. I think he suffers from *delusions of adequacy.*"

Van Oldag, the director of engineering who was typically very quiet, spoke up. "I'm not sure that Brady even knows where the factory is. I never see him there—he's always in his office working on charts. One of his worst ideas is his view on competition. He's having every department in a competition. Shearing is competing with stamping and stamping is competing with assembly. He even has the first shift competing with the second shift. It's creating a mess. In this company you can wind up being the winning member of the losing team. Brady is destroying whatever teamwork we used to have around here. I'll tell you one thing about this guy—he brings a lot of joy whenever he leaves a room."

Jim Willard, the cost accountant, spoke up. "This guy is the worst boss I've ever had. What I expect from a boss is simple. I want to be provided with the big picture, I want to be given a clear measurement system, and I want to be treated with respect. I get none of these. Everything is a big secret with this guy and I have no idea how his ratios, measurements, and confusing charts are supposed to help us solve any of our problems. Jim got up from his chair and started pacing the office waiving his arms. He went on, "The problems with Brady's metrics is that they are valueless for decision making. They are aggregated metrics that don't point to any root causes. I'll tell you how these kinds of metrics could push us to doing *wrong* things. Hey, Larry Smith, you want to improve your machine utilization score? It's one of Jim's favorites you know. Just stop all maintenance—the score will look really great. You can also improve your labor numbers—just stop all training. Unfortunately, that would be like pissing in your pants on a cold day to get warm. It would feel real good for three minutes, then it would get mighty cold."

It was clear that the team was going to have to come up with a plan to not only stop the losses but one that would recover them as well. They didn't even know where to begin. The only numbers they saw on a daily basis were total numbers of units produced as compared to a daily schedule. There was nothing that linked this to dollars. The group had no idea how to make up for a $150,000 loss. They certainly couldn't cut operating expenses by reducing staff and there was no overnight cure for the scrap and rework being produced by the workforce, most of whom were new and temporary.

"The number one problem around here," said Ellen "is our idiotic marketing department. The forecasts they issue are useless. Marketing constantly changes their forecasts so I spend all my time re-arranging production schedules and calling suppliers to either expedite or cancel orders. Our suppliers all think we're crazy. If marketing could be forced to freeze their schedule, we would have no problems in this factory."

Larry spoke up. "Marketing doesn't report to Jim and he's not going to let us get away with passing the blame onto Marketing. As for forecasts, as far as I'm concerned, there are two types of forecasts: *Lucky* and *Lousy*. I've never heard of a company with accurate forecasts. If these marketing people figure out a way of accurately forecasting, I suggest they all quit their jobs and spend their time at the racetrack. Our boss wants a plan and that's what we have to give him. A plan, not a list of excuses."

The team worked all day on a plan to eliminate their production backlog, increase output per person, and reduce defects. Their plan showed a steady improvement over a three-month period but none of them had any idea how to make it happen. It was 5:30 by the time they finished their plan. Larry decided to go home early that day. It was Friday night; maybe things would look better after the weekend. Larry missed his old job.

> *Fix the problem not the blame.*
>
> Japanese proverb

Discussion—From a LEAN management standpoint: What's going on in this chapter?

We have a real mess here. The factory performance is slipping badly, the staff hasn't a clue how to solve the problems, and they are all frightened and feel that their jobs are in jeopardy.

To make matters worse, the metrics available to them appear to be of no use.

One of the problems here is that the company is trying to solve their problem by focusing on improving their *results*. That's not going to get them far, unfortunately. Let me illustrate what I mean.

I live in Southern California. The house I live in came with an avocado orchard. Every year, the crop is harvested and I sell it to the local fruit growers cooperative. The more fruit harvested, the more money I get. I could, therefore, stand on my back porch every evening and scream at the trees something like, "Okay you damn trees, I want better results. I want 20% more avocados this picking season or I'll cut every one of you down!"

Sounds like a ridiculous thing to do, doesn't it? But is it any more ridiculous than what Jim Brady is doing to his staff? The only way they will get better results from their factory is to improve their processes. Improving processes creates improved results.

But how do processes get improved? Discovering where the waste is in those processes and permanently eliminating it improve processes.

- MANAGERS HAVE A LOT OF INFORMATION BUT IT IS USELESS AS FAR AS TELLING THEM WHAT THE PROBLEM MIGHT BE.
  - WHAT IS ROOT CAUSE? INFORMATION GIVES THEM NO IDEA.
- NONE OF THE INFORMATION IS RELATED.
- NOTHING SAYS MONEY LOSS IS TIED TO PRODUCTION OR EFFICIENCY.
  - PARTS SHORTAGE
  - REWORK
  - WASTE
- WORKING IN FEAR
- GOT A GUY REAL GOOD @ MAKING MEANINGLESS CHARTS.

CHAPTER 4

HUMILIATING DEFEAT

Larry spent the twenty-five-minute drive home replaying the events of the day in his mind. How did he let this happen to himself? He was perfectly content in his last job. Loved living in Oakdale. Had no pressure. And now here he is stuck in Fair Lawn where he doesn't know a soul, working for a son of a bitch and faced with a business problem that is beyond his ability to understand, let alone fix in six weeks.

He pulled into his driveway and was surprised to see his neighbor, Bob Simms, on his lawn talking to Sue. They were laughing at something Bob had said as Larry walked up to them. Bob looked relaxed and tan. How can somebody who runs a factory look so relaxed? When does he have time to get a tan like that?

"So Larry, I understand from Sue that you play tennis," said Bob Simms. "Want to play tomorrow morning?" "I would love to play tennis tomorrow," said Larry. He enjoyed the sport, was good at it, and had just bought a new racket in Oakdale before the job change. "I can't remember the last time I got some fresh air and exercise."

Bob Simms rang Larry's doorbell at 9:00 AM.

Larry was ready and looking forward to playing some tennis and getting to know Bob Simms. Maybe he could figure out Bob's secret. "He's either the boss's son or else he married the boss's daughter," thought Larry. Bob offered to drive to the courts. The BMW still smelled new.

Larry lost the match that mercifully took only thirty-four minutes. It seemed to Larry that Bob was hitting the ball effortlessly but he was shocked by how hard the balls Bob hit would strike his own racket. His immediate impulse was just to get out of the way not to get hit by the balls. Bob's serves were devastating. They looked to Larry as if they were served from so high that the balls were coming out of the sky at angles that made a return impossible. It seemed to Larry as if the balls would jump off the bounce to over his head or skew off to either side unpredictably. Even if Larry made a well placed offensive shot, Bob always seemed to be comfortably placed just on the right spot to respond. While Bob seemed to be playing a calm, almost effortless game, exerting a minimum of effort, Larry was exhausting himself running all over the court in useless attempts at returning balls that seemed as if they were being fired out of a high velocity cannon of some sort.

Larry was worn out; his body ached. He had never experienced such a defeat in tennis.

They walked back to Bob Simms's car. Bob popped the trunk and took out two ice cold mineral waters from a cooler. "Are you one of those guys who learned how to play tennis when you were three years old?" asked Larry. "No," replied

Simms, "this is only my second year." "How can that be? You play like a pro." said Larry.

Bob began to explain, "I took up tennis two years ago. Until then I never played at any sport seriously. I thought I lacked coordination. That was until I took trap shooting lessons." "What does trap shooting have to do with tennis?" asked Larry.

Larry greedily gulped at his bottle of water. Bob was taking small sips and stopped to answer Larry, "I've been trap shooting for the past twenty years. A friend of mine is fanatical about it and belongs to a shooting club. Twice a year he begs me to go with him. I was terrible at it but I agreed to go to his club mostly to be able to spend some time with the guy. Three years ago there was a note on the bulletin board at the club announcing private lessons for $15 per hour. So I gave it a try. The instructor was in his late sixties and had a fascinating teaching technique."

Bob continued with his explanation while sitting in the shade sipping his mineral water. There was no sign that he had just completed a tennis match. Larry was standing in the hot sun next to him looking as if he had just completed a marathon. Larry's water bottle was empty. Bob continued, "My trap shooting instructor's theory was that our body's ability is a lot better than we think. He explained to me that if you pointed at an object in the distance and there was a laser built into your pointing finger, that laser would point precisely at that object."

"On my first lesson, he gave me a BB gun and

told me that he was going to throw aspirins in the air and I was to shoot the aspirins with a BB. It seemed impossible. The bottle contained one hundred aspirins and I was somehow able to hit one aspirin. Then he brought out a second bottle and I hit three aspirins. We went through a dozen bottles that afternoon and by the last bottle I was able to hit forty out of the one hundred aspirins in the bottle. If I could hit an aspirin with a BB, hitting a clay pigeon with a pattern of shot is easy. I quickly became an outstanding trap shooter. That was the first time in my life I excelled at any sport."

"That motivated me to take up tennis. I figured that the reason I was never any good at trap shooting was I just wasn't relaxed enough. It was only after I relaxed and accepted the fact that our sports-playing ability is much, much better than we think it is and it's only after we really trust our own abilities that we can excel. It is like Yoda said in Star wars, 'You have to trust the force.' Our bodies have a built-in guidance system. All you need is a defined target and you must stop worrying about 'How?' What I learned about using up twelve bottles of aspirins is that it's okay to make mistakes and it's okay to forget past mistakes. It's like the rats in the maze—they learn from their errors in order to master the maze."

"Those trap-shooting lessons changed my life." Larry was shocked at the amount of passion Bob seemed to have over something as trivial as trap shooting. Bob continued, "I realized that I was so hung up on focusing on my form that I wasn't able to get good results. I thought about concert pianists. They don't stare at their fingers during the concert and worry about hitting the right keys. They've spent enough hours practicing and making mistakes so that now the keystrokes are each perfectly aimed and timed. The concert pianist ceases conscious efforts and relies on an *unconscious habit mechanism.* I then realized that the same lesson applies at work. My performance wasn't that good, I lacked courage to do anything risky and I was a nervous wreck. Once I figured out how to apply the lessons of the aspirin bottles to my job, my career soared and I was able to relax. I'm doing really well with my career."

"Emerson had a saying, 'Do the thing and you will have the power.' As I reflected on my pre-trap shooting behavior, I realized that I simply lacked *courage.* I now know that if you wait until you are certain before acting, you will never do anything. Once you move forward you can correct your course as you go. No guidance system works if you're standing still. I'm doing well, getting rich, and I'm more relaxed than ever."

"Well Bob," said Larry, "maybe you can relax in the stable bicycle parts business, but there's nothing to relax about at Sonic Loudspeakers." Now, in addition to hurting muscles, Larry started thinking about work and was developing a splitting headache. Larry continued, "I suppose I could use your attitude if not for the obnoxious ass I work for. I know that things are going to get better when our marketing forecasts improve. Right now I'm worried about keeping my job if I can't turn things around."

They drove back to Royal Hills and Bob pulled

into Larry's driveway to drop him off. "Larry my friend," said Bob, "if you don't mind my saying, I think you talk like a loser." "I'm not a loser," replied Larry. "I'm in a no-win situation."

Bob took out a laminated card from his wallet and showed it to Larry. The card contained three phrases:

√ If not for

√ When

√ What if

Bob went on to explain. "I carry this card in my wallet and make everyone that reports to me carry one. You can keep mine—I have lots more." Larry's calf muscles began to cramp painfully and his sweat-drenched shirt was stuck to the leather seatback. Simms showed no sign of having engaged in any physical activity. Every hair was in place and his posture quite relaxed. He continued, "These three phrases are the three things that losers say. They say they would be more successful 'if not for' the fact that they lack an Ivy League degree. They will be successful 'when' they get a new job. They are paralyzed with fear because 'what if' something goes wrong.

"Listen to yourself Larry," Bob went on as Larry began the excruciating task of pulling his aching body out of the Beemer, "You will be doing well '*if not for*' your boss. You will be doing well '*when*' forecasts improve. You worry about '*what if*' things don't improve. You sound like a victim.

Things will get better when you take charge of them. It's as simple as that."

"If you would like we can talk some more about this." Larry left Bob and walked into his house. He lost at tennis. Lost badly, and now was labeled as speaking the language of losers.

> *Some men see things as they are and ask, "Why?"*
> *I see things as they never were and ask, "Why not?"*
>
> John F. Kennedy

CHAPTER 5

THE CHALLENGE

The next week was pure hell for Larry. Jim Brady decided he had to take more control of the situation and announced that, until the crisis was over, he would conduct daily meetings that were to commence at 5:30 PM. Since the meetings were going to be lengthy, he would have pizza brought in. Larry didn't mind working long hours but these meetings were a waste of everyone's time. It was as if Brady were using the meetings as a form of punishment rather than a means of solving the problem.

Although they had submitted their get-well plan, nothing had changed. The material shortages continued, the high reject rate persisted, and the new improved numbers they committed to were not happening. As a matter of fact, performance was deteriorating even further. Jim Brady was getting more frustrated. He wore a perpetual scowl.

At Wednesday's meeting, Brady's secretary, Mary, brought in the pizza boxes and some side orders of salad. "What's in these boxes on top of the pizza, Mary?" asked Brady.

"Oh I thought it would be nice to have some salad along with your pizza," she answered. "You *thought* it would be nice?" Brady replied snidely. "Look, Mary, I don't pay you to think. I don't care what you think. If I wanted you to buy salad, I would have asked for it. Now is the time to put a lid on spending and not for clerks to make decisions on where the company's money should go." Mary's face turned red and looked like she was about to cry as she turned to leave the office.

Brady's evening meetings consisted of reviews of the day's numbers and commitments for improvements that were to take place the next day. Brady would take each of the day's performance numbers and convert them into complicated indexes that made no sense. He was tracking such things as labor efficiency and machine utilization and plotting them on daily charts. "So many charts" thought Larry, "There must be at least sixty. He must have his sex life tracking on one of them."

The "T" shaped arrangement made by the conference table intersecting the front of his desk dominated Brady's office. Charts—lots of charts— dominated the long wall. The wall behind his desk had two things on it, a large color portrait of him with his family and, next to that, his college degree. Larry had never seen an executive keep a college degree on an office wall. He had certainly seen degrees on doctors, lawyers and sometimes engineers, but never before in the office of an executive.

Brady would lead the meetings but there were very few discussions. Mostly there were sarcasm and threats from Brady. None of the committed improvements happened that week. Whenever it looked as if things were starting to get better, a new crisis would arrive. Machines would break down, wrong material was delivered, key trained people would call in sick, and one day the power from the utility company went down for two hours. Larry had never seen so many things go wrong at once.

Jim's attitude toward his team made it clear that he had little faith in their ability to straighten out the mess at Sonic. He told them he was speaking to a large consulting firm who gave him a quote on assessing his organization and implementing a production control system called Synchronized Demand. The quote also included installation of a conveyor system to bring parts from the warehouse into production.

By Friday night Larry was spent. He felt as if it would have been physically impossible for him to go into work on Saturday if he were called. He pulled into his driveway 7:00 PM Friday night and there was Bob Simms standing next to Sue. Bob and Sue were both laughing. Bob was wearing his tennis clothes, having obviously returned from a late afternoon game. There was no sign of sweat; every hair was in place. He had on a new pair of $200 sunglasses. Bob and Sue greeted Larry as he came out of his car. Larry's shirt was sweat stained and wrinkled, his pizza stained necktie partially undone. He was so drained that he could hardly stand up straight.

"Happy weekend, Larry," said Bob. "Are you ready for a re-match?" Bob asked Larry with a generous grin. "I don't think I'm ready for any-thing," answered Larry as he tried to straighten himself out. "This has been the worse week of my life." Sue gave Larry a hug and kiss and said, "The Simmses invited us to go out for pizza with them tonight and I thought that would be a great way to start the weekend." Larry responded quickly, "If I even look at another pizza I'll throw up. I've stayed late at work the last four nights at very difficult meetings conducted with my idiot boss who has been serving pizza to us. I've had so much pizza this week that I think my pimples are coming back."

"We don't have to have pizza," said Sue. "We could go to the sandwich shop by the lake. Go take a quick shower and we can be out of here in half an hour to start a relaxing weekend. Oh, and by the way, Jim Brady called here a few minutes ago to say he needed to tell you something." Larry couldn't believe it—he couldn't get away from Brady—not even on weekends.

One half hour later the two couples were in Bob's BMW on their way to the lake. Larry sat next to Bob in the front seat while their wives were in the back talking about their common enemy—the building contractor who had made too many prom-ises about fixing up the building defects that were discovered after the houses were moved into.

"Larry, you look like crap—if you don't mind my saying," said Bob. "Why are you so upset? he asked. Larry sunk into his seat and his head slumped forward. "Bob, I don't think I'm going to make it at Sonic. I don't think Sonic's going to make it. I can't believe how screwed up the place is. On top of all that, my boss may bring in a consulting firm to do an axe job and install a new production control system."

It was a lovely evening. The sun was setting. The sunset was starting to blossom and was going to be beautiful in a few minutes more. The country roads leading to the lake were picture-perfect. Bob expertly guided his magnificent, expensive, high-performance car through the turns. But all that was lost on Larry.

During the thirty-minute drive to the lake, Larry explained his situation to Bob. Bob kept quiet and just let Larry gush, figuring that he needed to get it out of his system. "Let me ask you something," said Bob as he took off his sunglasses now that they were no longer needed. "I have off on Monday; it's one of our two floating holidays. Would you like me to come visit your plant and see if I can offer some advice?" Larry was annoyed. He said to Bob, "I don't think this is one of those problems that can be diagnosed in the course of a one-hour visit. This is a complicated mess and the solution is going to be complicated as well."

Bob answered calmly, "Have you ever seen a doctor examine an x-ray? He doesn't ponder it for hours. He assesses the x-ray in a few moments. Or if you show a finance guy the books on a company—he very quickly sizes up the situation. Well, it's like that with factories. You can get a damn good assessment in an hour. I don't claim to be able to have all the answers, but I'm sure that I can help you understand the root causes of your situation and help you get a plan together to start putting permanent fixes in place. You don't have to tell your boss I'm coming. You must get lots of visitors."

Larry agreed to have Bob visit on Monday.

- LOOK FOR THE ROOT CAUSE -
- ASK THE 5 POINT QUESTION FOR EACH ISSUE -

CHAPTER 6

THE SENSEI

At 10:00 AM Monday morning, Larry was looking at the mountain of rework that was growing faster than it could be processed. He had completely forgotten that Bob Simms was going to visit until the receptionist called to say that Simms was in the front lobby waiting for him.

They walked into Larry's office. It was mid-morning and Larry was already distressed. Bob looked relaxed. Larry started to gather the charts to show Bob. "Larry, I don't care about charts; how about showing me around your factory. I'd like to tour the facility by starting at the shipping dock and walking the actual process flow that the product goes through, but in reverse order, back to your receiving department."

The tour lasted less than a half hour and then they returned to Larry's office.

"Larry, let me ask you a question" said Bob. "How long does your customer have to wait for his loudspeakers once he places an order?" Larry quickly answered, "Ninety days but lately it's taking over 120 days." "Okay, that's fine," continued Bob. "How long does it take from start to finish to make a loudspeaker?" "Fifty-one minutes," Larry quickly answered.

Bob leaned forward in his seat and pointed his finger at Larry and said, "Doesn't it seem strange to you that something that takes less than an hour to produce has a lead time of four months?"

"That's an interesting observation, Bob," said Larry, "but right now reducing lead times isn't what I'm being hammered about. My scrap rate is too high, my inventory turns are too low, my raw material warehouse is overloaded but I keep running out of parts. If all my parts were here and if Marketing could stop re-arranging my schedules, I would have no problems right now."

Simms quickly responded, "That's great Larry, and if I had wheels I would be a school bus." Simms stood up and was looking down at Larry who had slumped down into his chair. "Larry, my friend, you had better take charge of your situation and stop saying 'If not for this and if not for that things would be terrific.' If you don't make some changes fast, things will get a lot worse. It's like they say in the South, "If you keep *doin* what you've always done, you'll keep *gettin* what you always got."

"Things aren't as bad as you think they are. Your problem is simply this—there is no FLOW in your factory. What I see is a series of disjointed processes working at their own schedules, each pushing work-in-process to the next process. Work is supposed to flow through a factory like a river of water." Bob made a gesture with his arm showing a horizontal flow. "All movement is supposed to be horizontal. With all these shelves you have here, the material is flowing up and down. Up the shelves and then down the shelves. Work is being done in very large batches and I can see that whole batches are being rejected and then reworked. Work has to be done in the smallest possible batch sizes if you expect to get control over your production."

Larry protested, "You expect me to install a new production system? What am I supposed to use for money? I would have to organize all my suppliers—you're describing a project that would take years and my boss is breathing down my neck to solve this problem in the next few days."

Bob put his arm around Larry. "Look Larry, first of all, it's not going to cost anything to install a proper production system here. And you don't have to worry about your suppliers at this point. As for your boss, you can gain his support, but it's going to take some doing."

Bob took a form out of his briefcase and slid it across Larry's desk. "Your first step, Larry, is to make an assessment of the situation. I could give you my detailed analysis of the factory, but it's more important that you take a structured approach to analyzing your own situation. Let's fill this questionnaire out together. It won't take more than fifteen minutes but it will give you a quantified assessment of your problem areas and give you an idea of where to start."

The questionnaire was broken down into sections: JIT, Quality Achievement, Production Methods, Facility, Standards, and Personnel Management. Each section described a level of sophistication with a suggested point score for each description. (See Appendix A)

It took less than twenty minutes for Larry to fill out the form. Larry then slid the completed form back to Bob who took a summary sheet from his briefcase and filled it out for Larry. Bob then leaned back, handed the completed summary sheet back to Larry and asked, "Okay, Larry, here's your report card. Tell me what conclusions you can draw from it."

We trained hard but it seemed that every time we were beginning to form into a team we would reorganize.

I was to learn later in life that we tend to meet any new situation by reorganizing and a wonderful method it can be for creating the illusion of progress while producing confusion, inefficiency, and demoralization.

Petronius Arbiter 210 BC

MANUFACTURING EXCELLENCE SURVEY

Sonic Loudspeakers

Just In Time (JIT)	Score	Comments		
A. Layout (10 Pts.)	2			
B. Scheduling (20 Pts.)	3			
C. Maintenance (10 Pts.)	3			
D. Inventory Turns (20 Pts.)	3			
E. Lead Times (20 Pts.)	4		TOTAL	18
F. Metrics (10 Pts.)	1		OUT OF	100
G. Changeover (10 Pts.)	2		%	18%

Quality Achievement	Score	Comments		
A. Process Capability (20 Pts.)	3			
B. Quality Assurance (10 Pts.)	2			
C.Scrap & Rework (10 Pts.)	1			
D. Workmanship (10 Pts.)	1			
E. Measurement (10 Pts.)	1			
F. External Failure (10 Pts.)	1		TOTAL	22
G. Supplier Quality(10 Pts.)	7		OUT OF	100
H. Customer Satisfaction (20 Pts.)	6		%	22%

Production Methods	Score	Comments		
A. Work Flow(20 Pts.)	2			
B. Inventory (20 Pts.)	2			
C. Rework(10 Pts.)	3			
D. Process Status (10 Pts.)	2		TOTAL	18
E. Cell Technology (20 Pts.)	3		OUT OF	100
F. Automation(20 Pts.)	6		%	18%

Facility	Score	Comments		
A. House Keeping(20 Pts.)	3			
B. Traffic(10 Pts.)	2		TOTAL	13
C. Storage(10 Pts.)	3		OUT OF	50
D. Condition (10 Pts.)	5		%	26%

Standards	Score	Comments		
A. Process(20 Pts.)	3		TOTAL	11
B. Work Instructions(20 Pts.)	5		OUT OF	50
C. Information(10 Pts.)	3		%	22%

Personnel Management	Score	Comments		
A. Labor Relations(20 Pts.)	10			
B. Organization (10 Pts.)	7			
C. Leadership(20 Pts.)	0			
D. Work Practice (10 Pts.)	3		TOTAL	24
E. Motivation(20 Pts.)	2		OUT OF	100
F. Development(20 Pts.)	2		%	24%

			TOTAL	106
			OUT OF	500
TOTAL SCORE			%	21.2%

Manufacturing Excellence Survey Summary

Larry studied the summary form carefully and concluded, "Well first of all, I see that my whole factory only scored 21.2% and that would be a failing score in any school. Second, it looks like there's not one area that doesn't need fixing."

Bob smiled and rubbed his stomach saying, "You know Larry, I'm getting hungry and would like to take you to lunch but I want to finish this conversation first. But speaking of lunch, Larry—do you know how to eat an elephant?" Larry looked puzzled. "Well Larry, there's only one way to eat an elephant and that's one bite at a time. And that's the way you have to go about fixing this factory. So where do you think the first bite has to be taken?"

Larry studied the summary form again and said, "All the scores are low—too low—but I'd say the areas of JIT and production methods have to come first." Bob smiled broadly and said, "Okay, but the area of production methods is an elephant in itself. Which is the first bite you can take of that elephant, Larry?"

Larry took out the detail sheets, studied them for a minute and concluded, "Work Flow has a score of 2 out of 20—that looks like a good place to start, but how should I start? I can't rearrange my factory. I'm behind on every order today and if I stop to do a rearrangement I'll only fall further behind. It would be like trying to change all the tires on a car while going sixty miles per hour."

"It's not that bad," said Bob, "I'll tell you a simple way to do it but I've got to get some lunch.

Is there a restaurant around here we can go to?"
"Not so fast, Bob" Larry said. "I want to hear how
I can improve the work flow in my 21% factory
without spending a fortune and without falling
further behind. I suppose what you're going to
suggest is that I find the constraint in my factory
and remove it so that I can get some sort of flow
going."

Bob snapped back, "Launching an attack on
your constraint right now would be a waste of time.
First of all, by increasing the throughput of your
constraint, you could wind up creating even more
work-in-process and actually increasing your leadtime. And secondly, if you were able to fix your
biggest bottleneck, all that would create would be
an *isolated victory* but the overall situation would
be unchanged. You need a quantified understanding of the flow through your entire factory, from
incoming materials through to shipping. You also
need to understand to what extent your production control system is causing a lot of your shortages."

Bob rose from his seat, "I'll get you started,
that's why I came here to visit you. Get some paper and let's go out in the factory. That's where
the opportunity is, not here in this office. I'm going to help you draw a simplified Value Stream
Map." Bob and Larry toured the factory once more
starting with the shipping dock and working their
way back to the incoming materials dock. Bob and
Larry drew a very simple flow chart with a box
representing each process that the product went
through. These included incoming inspection,
shearing, stamping, assembly and test. He had

Larry estimate the amount of work in process between each process that he wrote in each box. He then had Larry estimate the cycle time of each process and write that number in the individual process boxes.

No one is useless in the world who lightens the burden of it for anyone else.

C. Dickens

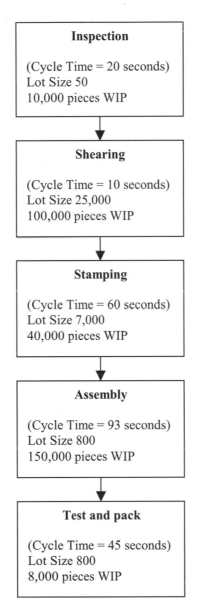

Factory Flow

It took no more that a half hour for Larry and Bob to walk the route that the product took through the factory and to sketch the route along with cycle times and WIP on a single piece of paper. They then returned to Larry's office to study the paper.

Bob pointed to the "Shearing" box. "Look here, Larry. You have an inventory of 100,000 pieces between shearing and the stamping operation. If it takes thirty seconds to stamp the part, that means that each piece has to wait *months* between processes."

"That's impossible," protested Larry. "The press is the most efficient machine we own. It can't be a bottleneck." Bob took his pencil and did a quick calculation for Larry. "Look here, Larry—if you divide the 100,000 pieces that are waiting for the press and divide that by the half minute the press takes to process the parts you get 50,000 minutes of work. If you divide that by the 420 available working minutes in a shift, you get 119 days. Since you work the presses on two shifts, that's 59 working days—almost three months."

"A more sensible way to look at it is with Takt Time," Bob explained. Larry stopped him, "I don't know what Takt Time means." Bob continued, "Takt is a German word meaning beat, like heartbeat. A factory has a beat and that beat is called the Takt Time. It is calculated by dividing the available time in a day by the customer demand. For example, you told me you need to make 800 units a day of the typical model. Working two shifts gives you 840 available minutes a day. Divide 840 minutes a day by the demand of 800 units tells you that your takt time is 1.05 minutes per piece. Your 100,000 pieces at the Takt Time rate of 1.05 minutes each will take 95,238 minutes of work to consume. At 840 minutes a day, that's 113 days—five and one half months.

Takt Time = <u>Available minutes per day</u>
              Customer demand

Takt Time = <u>8 hours per shift x 60 mins per hour –</u>
              <u>(30 min. lunch+(2) 15 min breaks) x 2 shifts</u>
              800 Units

Takt Time = <u>840 minutes per day</u> = 1.05 min/piece
              800 Units

Time to Consume Inventory = <u>Inventory</u>
                              Takt Time

Time to Consume =   <u>100,000 pieces</u> =
                      1.05 Min/Piece

              =   <u>95,238 Minutes</u> =
                  840 Min/Day

              =   **113 Days**

Larry saw Bob staring at the row of racks of 100,000 sheared parts waiting to be stamped. Larry asked Bob why he was looking at the parts. "Let me ask you something Larry. Why on earth do you have so many sheared parts here?"

Larry explained, "I have no choice to have a buffer of inventory after my shearing and blanking machines. First of all, these machines are ancient and keep breaking down unexpectedly. Sometimes it takes as much as four hours to get them going again. If I don't have a buffer stock here, I could shut down my whole operation.

Bob pointed to the box on the paper showing the inventory level after stamping. "Okay, I understand why you have a 100,000 buffer stock after shearing. It's because your old machines are breaking down. But you show 40,000 pieces after the stamping operation. Stamping presses are typically pretty reliable. Why do you have so much inventory after stamping?"

Larry replied, "Actually the main reason for the buffer is the long setup time on the press. It could take as long as six hours to set the machine up. It's really a trial and error type thing. I'm not going to spend all day setting up the press and then just run it for an hour or two."

Bob continued, "Now Larry don't go off on some mission to speed up the presses because it looks like a constraint. What you have to do now is go back and get some good data. All we have now is rough estimates. When you go back and collect data, add some more detail to each box.

Write down how long the setups are at each stage, what the lot sizes are and be sure to write down what the people were doing at each station. Were they working, idle, receiving instructions, getting material, searching for tools, whatever?

"Take a few days to re-do this analysis thoroughly and then you and I can sit down together and map out a strategy to fix this mess. There's another reason for all this work-in-process inventory that we haven't even discussed yet. Your boss, Brady, likes the idea of competition. He is pitting each department against one another. Each department is working as fast as they possible can, mainly to make their numbers look good. What we see is the result of managing for *local efficiency*. If instead this place was managed for *global efficiency*, each department would only produce what the next department needed.

"I know you've seen crew style boating races. Each rower pulls at the same pace. If one of those rowers pulled harder than all the rest, the boat wouldn't win any races. Your boat is going around in circles while you build inventory between operations.

"Let's get together Wednesday night at my house after work and we can put a plan together in two hours. Now I'm really hungry—let's get some lunch."

Discussion—From a LEAN management standpoint: What's going on in this chapter?

Larry learned two important things in this last chapter. He learned that his greatest opportunity was to improve his flow. And he learned that it would be a mistake to launch an attack on what he perceived to be the factory's constraint.

Long before the world learned about Lean manufacturing and long before Toyota invented what we now call "Just-in-Time," Henry Ford developed a manufacturing method to tremendously reduce the cost of manufacturing his automobiles. What springs to the average mind is his use of the conveyorized assembly line. But it was something more fundamental that made his factory so efficient. It was Henry Ford's obsession with improving flow.

A famous quote by Ford is, "One of the most noteworthy accomplishments in keeping the price of Ford products low is the gradual shortening of the production cycle. The longer an article is in the process of manufacture and the more it is moved about, the greater is its ultimate cost."

The remarkable thing about that quotation is that Ford said it in 1926. What is truly remarkable is how good the flow in his factory was. Ford factories were vertically integrated back then. Ford owned the iron mines that produced the ore that his car's steel used. He owned the forests that provided the wood for the car body frames. He even owned the rubber plantations that provided the rubber for Ford tires.

The Ford plant was situated on a river in Michigan so that barges could deliver his raw materials. If iron ore was unloaded at the dock at 7:00 PM on a Monday evening, by noon on Wednesday that iron ore had been converted into an automobile sitting in a Michigan showroom. Ford realized, even back then, that one of the most critical metrics to improve in manufacturing is *velocity*.

Ford not only focused on flow, he focused on continuous improvement of flow. As a result he was able to reduce the selling price of his cars from year-to-year in the 1920s.

The second thing Larry learned is that he can't rush headlong into improving things without understanding his company's *system*.

Larry studied engineering in college. One thing that is drilled into the heads of engineering students is that every element that we study is one part of a system and if you want to improve the element, you must understand where and how it fits into that system.

Attacking the area that Larry considers his constraint could result in creating more work- in-process inventory. Furthermore, it has been proven many times that companies that attack one department at a time without a comprehensive total system success plan wind up with islands of excellence which if not linked together, make little difference to the bottom line.

CHAPTER 7

YIN AND YANG

Bob drove Larry to an Italian restaurant near the Sonic factory. They slid into a booth and Bob tossed his car keys and sunglasses on the checkered tablecloth.

"Hey, Bob," asked Larry, "how come you have that medallion on your key chain? I've seen teenagers with buttons like that but never understood what it stood for."

Bob's face got serious as he reached for the medallion and held it—almost caressed it. "This isn't kid stuff," said Bob. "Remember when I told you that my trap shooting instructor changed my outlook on a lot of things? Well, there was another man that influenced me. He was a Kaizen consultant at the last place I worked. Kaizen is the Japanese expression for continuous improvement. Kaizen is a Japanese approach to achieving continuous improvement by eliminating waste. This guy was terrific. He studied Kaizen in Japan, 'Americanized' it, and used the technique to bring about amazing improvements very quickly to clients he consulted for.

"This consultant used the Yin and Yang symbol on his business card and one day he explained its significance."

Larry interrupted, asking, "Doesn't it have something to do with opposites attracting, or the balance of the earth, or something like that?"

Bob continued. "The symbol is two fishes. A black fish with a white eye and a white fish with a black eye. There's a sort of "S" shape separating the fish. The symbol represents the universe. The "S" shape shows that things are always in motion" Bob made a sweeping, smooth big "S" gesture with his hand. "So you can say that the two fish represent opposites like night and day or like hard and soft or like man and woman or like truth and lies. But see the "S" shape, it symbolizes change. It's like day changes to night and then back to day.

"One of the secrets to success and happiness is the ability to *cope* with change. In the business world, it's the companies that don't face up to change who go out of business. You and I know that if Sonic doesn't make some serious changes quickly, they won't survive. In order to cope with change, there is a requirement that we can let go of the past. Companies that don't let go of their past—their paradigms—are incapable of improvement.

In a more global interpretation it could represent countries. One day a country like Japan is on top and the U.S is in a recession. Then that changes and the opposite is true." Bob made a gesture with his hands as if he were holding an invisible volleyball with one hand on top and one on the bottom. He switched his hands by rotating the ball one hundred and eighty degrees to illustrate the point he had just made. "Another example is politics in the workplace and I know you've seen this, Larry. One day some guy is on top, running everything and the next day he's out the door and some guy he had been tormenting is on top, replacing his tormentor." Larry liked the sound of that and relished the image for a few moments.

Bob continued, "The symbol teaches us that change is constant. Companies that don't change don't last. Think back to the 60s when IBM, GM, and Sears were on top. They ignored the changes happening before their eyes. GM ignored Toyota, Sears ignored Wal-Mart, and IBM ignored PC's. They were the white fish and they became the black fish because they were unable to change. That's what will happen at Sonic if you don't change.

"There's another interesting part of the symbol and that's the different color eyes in the fish. Let's say that the black fish represents lies and the white fish represents truth. You know that within every lie there is some truth. And similarly, every truth has a little bit of lie in it. Or to put it another way, think about your boss who you have so much resentment for. He's the black fish. He's not totally useless, is he? I'll bet he has lots of qualities you admire and might even be a little jealous of.

"Let me give you more of the symbolism. Let's say that the black fish represents men and the white fish represents women. In that case the entwined fish could be symbolic of how women nurture and embrace their men." Bob made a gesture with his arms as if he were holding an invisible child. "The man—the black fish—he's tough, he's in charge. But think of most families: who is in charge, the tough man or the compliant, embracing woman? It's like in nature, with the black fish representing rocks and the white fish representing water. Which gets worn down? The soft water always prevails. And like women, water could freeze and get very tough and do great damage.

"All this symbolism translates into a useful business philosophy. First of all, there's a lot to be learned from the compliance of women. The tough, confrontational boss isn't likely to be effective in the long run. The boss who takes on what you may call feminine characteristics is the one that will prevail. It's the nurturing, forgiving boss that will lead the successful organization.

"If you've studied any martial arts you know that the most effective tactic is a withdrawal. Attacking an opponent who is racing at you only results in a painful and useless collision. But the fighter who is withdrawing is the one in control of his opponent's moves. During the withdrawal, he can study his opponent's positions and can notice things like the fact that his attacker spreads his legs whenever he raises his left arm. This allows the person withdrawing to kick his attacker in the groin the next time he raises his left arm. Head-on confrontation rarely produces anything useful."

Bob and Larry had subs. Larry tasted nothing and wished he could have a beer with his lunch but knew that would result in a sleepy afternoon.

Larry wiped his mouth after finishing his sandwich and said to Bob, "You mentioned the word
Kaizen. I don't know if any of that stuff really
works. Back at my old company I read a book on
5S—a Japanese approach to industrial housekeeping. I launched a program to clean the place up.
We put stripes on all the aisles, made places for
everything and made sure that everything was in
its place. When we finished the place looked fantastic. But within six weeks, the place reverted
back to being a mess. I then read a book about
Kaizen; it was nothing but abstract philosophy—
nothing about *how* to do Kaizen. The book had
lots of case studies with before and after photos
but I had no idea how these companies organized
their efforts or what kind of training the teams
needed before they started."

Bob looked stunned. "Larry, my man, could
you read a book about the history of tennis and
be any good at the sport? A lot of the books on the
market lack the detail of implementation. As for
your 5-S fiasco, that's the problem with *programs*.
The workforce treat programs passive- aggressively
and will go through the motions until management
gets bored like they always do and come up with
the next program—the next *flavor of the month*.

They finished lunch and agreed to meet at
Bob's house Wednesday after dinner. Larry got
back to his office and found a note on his chair
from Brady, asking Larry to come to his office.
Brady had three men with him. The most senior
looking of the three was distinguished and could
have passed for a fifty year-old male model. The
guy had a great silvery head of "executive hair"

and what looked to Larry like polished fingernails. His two associates looked like youngsters straight out of their MBA schools.

Brady introduced Larry to the three visitors and explained that they were from SDI, Synchronized Demand International, a consulting firm specializing in installing a very expensive production control system and reorganizing staffs. Larry was amazed at how charming and friendly Brady could be to strangers. It was as if the guy had two different personalities, one for his staff and the other for the outside world. What a snake!

Brady asked Larry to give the men a complete tour of the facility so they could collect data for preparation of a proposal. Brady agreed to pay $7,500 for the proposal but the money would be refunded if a contract were awarded to SDI.

Larry took the two *kids* on the tour while the senior guy stayed in Brady's office. Larry noticed as he was leaving Brady's office that Brady had his file of organizational charts on his desk. There was no mystery about what that discussion would be about. Larry felt sick.

The tour took five hours. The young consultants took detailed notes of their factory observations and asked if they could go to Larry's office and review inventory level records of raw material, work-in-process, and finished goods.

Afterward, Larry took the two of them back to Brady's office. It was now 7:30 PM. Brady and the senior consultant were still at it. Brady had organization charts and financial statements spread across his conference table. Larry envisioned Brady trying to convince the senior consultant to review his wall of charts. Larry assumed that the seasoned consultant knew better than to get roped into looking at useless charts and steered the analysis towards available financial records.

The senior guy looked up when Larry and his two men entered the room. "Well guys," he said as he got up from the conference table, "I hope you two had as productive an afternoon as Jim and I just had. I figure we could save this company at least $1.5 million a year in inventory reduction, improved throughput, improved customer service, and reduced floor space." One of the two guys that Larry had in tow spoke up. "I figure another $500,000 a year in reduced scrap, rework, and improved labor efficiency. This place is the perfect candidate for our new Synchronized Demand software."

Larry thought to himself "these guys are pulling numbers out of the air. I don't need a software program that will take nine months to implement. I need to do something fast to get this constipated factory flowing."

> *An individual without information*
> *cannot take responsibility.*
> *An individual who is given information*
> *cannot help but take responsibility.*
>
> Jan Carlson

Discussion—From a LEAN management standpoint: What's going on in this chapter?

Bob Simms has begun his role as *Sensei*. The word *Sensei* is Japanese and originally was defined as "teacher of martial arts." It has evolved to mean "teacher or master" in general.

The role of the industrial sensei in Japan versus the West is a bit different, however.

I was introduced to Lean manufacturing and Kaizen techniques in Tokyo, Japan, where I attended the Kaizen Institute. That experience changed my life.

The Kaizen Institute was originally located in Washington, DC, in the early 1950s. They created a school where Japanese manufacturing managers could learn Western production techniques and then be taken on tours of the best American factories.

I learned about the Kaizen Institute in 1992. By then they were no longer located in Washington. They moved to Tokyo where they held classes for Western managers and took them on tours of Japanese factories that had won the prestigious Deming prize.

My class make-up consisted of two Americans, one Englishman and forty managers from the Porsche factory in Germany. The year was 1992 and Porsche was going broke and contemplating shutting down completely.

We had signed up for a two-week course. The first week was strictly classroom lecture and trips to the Deming award factories. The second week was spent in an actual Kaizen event in the factory where the Isuzu Trooper was being made.

The classroom lectures were delivered in Japanese by authorities in various Lean disciplines. We all wore earpieces that received simultaneous English translations from the interpreters located in the rear of the room. These lectures lasted about four hours. We were then taken by bus to factories where we could see in person the application of the principles of the morning lecture.

After the week of theory, we were ready for a real Kaizen event. Our class was taken to the Isuzu factory where we joined a meeting. The general manager had assembled about one hundred employees. He announced that Trooper sales were soaring and he needed a 20% increase in output *in the next three days*. It was understood that very little money was to be spent on these improvements and that all improvements had to be put in place within the three days. He said that he wanted a formal presentation at the end of the three-day period to hear about our success. The pressure was on.

The challenge sounded impossible to my classmates and me. Isuzu had hired one of our instructors from the Institute to lead this Kaizen event. The Isuzu employees were split into about fifteen teams. Our class was dispersed into each of these Kaizen teams. Isuzu was very experienced in conducting Kaizen events. All the team members had been on many prior events and were very familiar with the tools. That's why this was only a three day event as compared to the West where a project of this type would take five days.

Each team was assigned to a different section of the factory. My team of five people was assigned to the drive shaft assembly. The assembly consisted of the shaft which had to be cut to size and then had universal joints welded to each end. At the end of the three days we were able to apply the Kaizen principles to successfully increase output by 25%.

The other teams had similar results. I was astounded by the results. It really didn't seem possible at first.

I mentioned that this was an experience that changed my life. That's because I was able to bring these techniques back to successfully apply them to my own company in America where I was employed. And that led to establishment of my international consultancy.

My intention here, however is to describe the role of the sensei. In the West, our sensei's— our masters—are viewed as coaches. They are supportive, encouraging, and often use a Socratic approach to teaching. That is, they teach by asking provocative questions that force the students to come to the proper conclusion on their own.

This was not the approach of our sensei on that Kaizen event. He walked among the fifteen teams throughout the three days making sure we were on track. But the unsettling thing was his treatment of us. My team members said, "we don't think of him as a consultant—we think of him as an "Insultant." And insulting he was indeed throughout the three days. But they loved the guy.

I was later to learn that many American firms hired Japanese Kaizen consultants to help them with their Lean conversions in the 1990s. Those Japanese consultants that tried the Insultant approach were often thrown out of the American factories. We don't like being insulted.

At the end of the three-day Kaizen event we had to make a formal presentation to the general manager of the Isuzu plant. All the teams worked late into the night in preparation of the presentation.

The accomplishment was something we were very proud of. After the presentation, the general manager thanked the teams for their hard work for the past three days and gave us our well-deserved congratulations for giving him the 20% increase he tasked us to achieve.

He then turned the meeting over to our leader, the insultant. True to his reputation, he proceeded to blast us with criticism about how much better we *could have done.* My Japanese teammate leaned over to me during the tirade and said, "Isn't he terrific!"

Although the style of the insultant is hard for us to take, he is doing something very important. I have tremendous respect for these individuals.

They are truly manufacturing geniuses and very effective teachers. In the West we celebrate the successful achievement of the goals at the end of a Kaizen event. We even celebrate if the goals aren't completely achieved. The Japanese approach is different. Even when the Kaizen team meets the expectations, they critically analyze what they had just done and ask, "How could it have been even better?" In the spirit of continuous improvement, they Kaizen the Kaizen.

As everyone now knows, Porsche took the lessons of the Kaizen Institute back to their plant and successfully applied them to their German factory. Application of these techniques and hiring insultants to come to Germany changed the fate of Porsche, which is now a profitable company and producing cars with fewer defects than ever before.

CHAPTER 8

CREATING THE SUCCESS PLAN

Larry walked across the street to Bob Simms's house after dinner Wednesday evening. Larry had been in a mental fog after spending time with the consultants. He couldn't concentrate on his job when he was at work and then at home he didn't really hear anything his wife or kids were saying to him. He had pretty much assumed that Jim Brady would hire SDI and the new organization chart wouldn't have his name on it.

Lesley Simms answered the door to let Larry in. While still at the doorway, Larry could hear Simms and his kids laughing as they played a board game together. Larry wished he had the stability in his life to be able to enjoy his family—to be able to enjoy anything,

Bob and Larry went into Bob's home office. He had never seen this room before. A photograph on the wall of Bob shaking hands with Ronald Reagan struck Larry. Larry got up close to the picture and asked, "Were you and Reagan friends?"

Bob walked over to the picture, an obvious treasure to him. "I wouldn't call us friends exactly but I will say that he's my personal hero." Larry was impressed and continued to be amazed at

Simms's lifestyle and personal philosophy. The office was loaded with fascinating stuff. Larry wanted to just walk around it and look at all the stuff Bob had on display. He had an antique globe that stood on a floor stand. An internal bulb illuminated the globe. Next to that was a bookstand that looked like a speaker's podium. It supported an enormous dictionary. He had a wall cabinet with a display of restored antique revolvers. The walls were covered with photos Bob had taken of his favorite adventure vacations.

Bob and Larry sat down at the oversized desk where Bob laid the paperwork Larry had prepared. It looked like the bottleneck was, in fact, the presses. The problem was the setup time. It was taking an average of 90 minutes to do the setup. Sonics had a calculation done in the accounting department that mandated the lot size for the press to be 7,000 pieces.

Bob added up the "touch-time" for his product—that is, the total minutes actually required producing the product, the time the product was actually being worked on—not including the time it was waiting for the next process.

Operation	Cycle Time	Setup Time	Lot Size (Pcs)	Inventory (Pcs)
Inspection	23 Sec.	0 Min.	50	10,700
Shear & Blank	12 Sec.	45 Min.	25,000	100,560
Stamp	56 Sec.	90 Min.	7,000	82,567
Assembly	96 Sec.	0 Min.	-	152,500
Test and Pack	27 Sec.	0 Min.	-	-
TOTAL	214 Sec.			346,327

Bob looked at these numbers and asked Larry, "What do these numbers tell you?" Larry shot back, "They tell me four very important things. First of all, I now know that it takes only 214 seconds to process a part. But I know how long it really takes a part to get from the incoming dock to the outgoing dock—about two months. It looks like we have *a velocity* problem."

"The second thing these numbers tell me is that my bottleneck is the assembly department. I have one piece coming off the assembly line every 96 seconds but my Takt Time, my customer demand, is 63 seconds.

"The third thing I see is that I have one hell of an opportunity to reduce the work-in-process inventory at my shears and presses if I could only reduce downtime on the shears and improve setup times on the presses.

"The fourth thing really surprised me. I knew we had a lot of WIP in the assembly department but I had no idea there were over 150,000 pieces.

The company's logic had always been that we need lots of inventory to supply the assembly department because we have to be able to respond to our customers' demand for every one of our products. Our Marketing department has been unable to forecast which products are most likely to be ordered, so our strategy was to stockpile every part in a ready-to-assemble condition."

Bob was smiling; he stood up and patted Larry on the back. "So taking a few hours out to do a simple analysis paid off for you. I think we could put together a success plan tonight that will make you very happy. Let me talk to you about setup times."

"Larry," Bob continued, "If you had to leave my house this second and immediately begin the task of getting four new tires put on your car, filling the gas tank to the top, cleaning the windshield, and then drinking seven ounce of water, how long would you guess that would take?" Larry thought for a few seconds, his eyes looking up at the ceiling as if the answer were written there and said, "I suppose I could do it in two hours."

Bob then said, "Now hold onto that thought and let me ask you a second question. Which car in the Indianapolis 500 race wins?" Larry immediately answered, "The fastest car wins I suppose." "Well, Larry," answered Bob, "you don't know much about car races. Actually, it's not always the fastest car that wins. It usually is the car that spends the least amount of time in the pit. And what happens in the pit? That's where they replace all four tires, fill the gas tank, clean the windshield and give the driver seven ounces of water to drink. And how long do you think that takes? Would you believe less than nine seconds?

"There are three reasons all that stuff gets done in less than nine seconds. First, the pit *process* was continuously improved over time. Second, the team knows how to *work well together* (or maybe their leader knows how to get them to work well together). And third, the team *practices*. I'm going to tell you how the setup time on that lathe is going to get cut down a lot. But first I want to tell you how upset I am about your boss even considering hiring consultants and paying a fortune to install a Synchronized Demand System. I know that's the latest panacea to come along.

"Experts have come along since the start of the industrial revolution, claiming to have the one and only secret to business success. These panaceas have come and gone for the past 100 years. While it is reckless to embrace any one technique as the answer to all your business problems, there are elements from all of them that are excellent. The latest technique is called, 'Lean.' The term comes to us from Japan and was first described to Americans in a book published in 1990 called *The Machine That Changed the World*. In this book by authors James Womack, Daniel Jones, and Daniel Roos, they describe Japanese management practices that enabled their stunning success in the automotive and consumer electronics businesses.

Bob explained further, "When 'Lean' companies are compared to ordinary companies, we see these differences: Lean companies take *half* the human effort; Lean companies have one-half the defects in the finished product (or *service*); Lean companies require one-third the engineering effort; Lean companies use half the floor space for the same output; Lean companies have 90% less inventory.

"There are quite a few companies in the U.S. today who are considered Lean. These people are thankful they took the effort to begin the *changes* that resulted in their transformation. We don't like changing and we avoid it. But there comes a point where we are so disgusted with the existing situation that we begin the way down that difficult path. One example is dieting. We tend to ignore the slowly increasing girth until that one painful day when we get a glimpse of our naked self in the mirror. "Is that really me? THAT'S IT—I'm on a diet starting right now!' Or the slowly creeping credit card balance. One day we open that envelope and say, 'How the hell did I accumulate so much debt—I must have been nuts. THAT'S IT—I'm on a tight budget starting right now!'

"I think that you, Larry, are certainly at that point at Sonic."

Bob's wife, Lesley, then came into the office with two frosty mugs of beer. "I thought you boys would like these; it looks like you're gonna be here awhile."

Larry accepted the beer eagerly and sat back in the chair while Bob continued. Bob sounded like a college professor now but Larry wished he had professors like that back in college.

"The journey down the path to becoming Lean in business starts with the leader, and it takes a strong leader. This leader realizes three things: there are no quick fixes (or panaceas); his business probably won't survive unless it changes the way they do business; the situation requires a revolution.

"Effective leaders know that dramatic improvement cannot be made by 'exhortation.' It takes a lot more than inspirational speeches, incentives, or threats. Your boss is certainly threatening you and it doesn't seem to be getting him anywhere.

"Larry, you and your boss are going to have to lead the change in that factory and the change must begin with your "call to action." Everyone in the organization needs to know that the business cannot continue operating the way it does—it won't survive; everyone must change the way they do their jobs. Everyone!

"The problem is what to change and how to change. An effective method could be to bring in an outsider who won't miss the forest for the trees. A very useful technique for bringing about change very quickly is called Kaizen. Kaizen is a Japanese word meaning *continuous improvement* and is the most common technique for creating the Lean Enterprise. Application of Kaizen involves a study of the businesses processes in an effort to discover where the waste is. Then a new process is implemented after all the waste has been removed. The amazing thing about Kaizen is the speed of implementation.

"There are lots of consulting companies like the Synchronized Demand Institute who pour expensive teams into the client's company and spend months gathering data. This data gathering culminates in a fancy report chocked full of terrific ideas. The report often resides on the boss's desk and the terrific ideas never get implemented.

"Kaizen uses a technique called the blitz. The blitz can be conducted by an outside consultant or one of your own people trained in the techniques. The strategy is to select one process in the company to improve. A blitz takes 3-5 days. A team of 6-12 people from across the organization is formed and given one full day of training in techniques to identify and eliminate waste. The focus of the team could either be a factory or an administrative function. Then the team spends the rest of their time implementing the new, vastly improved process.

"At the conclusion of the week, not only has a key business process been improved very quickly, but a team has been trained that can apply this same technique to other processes in the company. Unlike other improvement methods, Kaizen provides very quick implementation; is low cost since it relies on your own people, not a gang of expensive young consultants; implants an effective team approach to problem solving and process improvement.

"Once the decision is made to use Kaizen, the next critical decision is to select a process to dramatically improve. The process selected to improve should have the following attributes: it should currently be dysfunctional; improving it should make customers happy (and competitors worry); it should have a high likelihood of being success-fully improved.

"One of the techniques employed by Kaizen practitioners is to reduce setup times in factories. Toyota, for example, was able to reduce the time to changeover their presses from producing one type of fender to another from twelve hours to nine minutes. Our initial example compared your esti-mate of changing four tires in two hours to that of the professional team who does it in seconds. The pros do it without all the waste. The waste was removed from their process.

"I think I would like to spend a week in your plant as your Kaizen consultant. I'll use one of my vacation weeks. I really want to do this for you, Larry."

Larry was dumbfounded. "Bob, I can't ask you to give me one of your vacation weeks. And even if I agreed to do this, I don't have a budget to pay you for our services."

Bob took a long sip of his beer and said to Larry, "I won't charge you a cent; this is some-thing I really want to do. I get a kick out of doing these things. I thought you would be jumping up at this point and thanking me. Why are you look-ing so puzzled?"

Larry looked bewildered. After a long pull on

his beer he finally responded. "Listen, Bob, I am enormously grateful for your offer, but I don't view this as a one-week project. I think it would be easier to boil the ocean than turn this mess around. These problems would take years to fix. I have to decrease my setup times, eliminate the bottlenecks in the assembly department, and introduce Just-in-Time to the company."

Bob stood up, walked around his desk, stood next to Larry and put an arm on his shoulder. "Listen, Larry, it's not as hard as you think. I can spend a week in your facility doing Kaizen with your people. We could form two teams that I would lead. One team would be assigned to reduce setup times in fabrication and the second team would be assigned to radically improving the assembly department. Both teams will also work together to install a Just-in-Time delivery system." "Hold it right there," Larry interrupted. "You've got to be kidding about installing a Just-in-Time system. Install JIT in one week? I don't think so!"

"Larry, come with me—I'll show you a JIT system in Lesley's kitchen," Bob said as he led Larry to the Simms kitchen. It was now 9:00 PM, the kitchen was cleaned up from the evening's dinner. Lesley was in the adjacent family room reading a book.

The two men were standing in the middle of the kitchen. Bob turned to Larry and asked, "Larry, what do you see in this kitchen?"

"I see a neat kitchen. Is there something I'm missing?" asked Larry.

"I'll tell you what you're missing," began Bob. "You're missing the best example of a highly successful JIT system. First of all, notice that Lesley's kitchen is spotlessly clean. At the end of every meal, she scrubs everything clean and restores everything to where it belongs. There is a place for everything and everything is in its place. Look where Lesley located her tools. The knife rack is adjacent to the butcher block. The spice rack is next to the counter where she mixes her ingredients and her mixing bowls are right under the counter.

"Before each meal she plans the sequence of operations so that the entire meal is delivered to the dining room table 'just in time.' She knows that the baked potatoes must go into the oven 30 minutes before the fish, for example. Otherwise she would serve the potatoes 15 minutes after we finish desert.

"Let's compare Lesley's kitchen to your factory. You certainly don't have a place for everything and everything in its place. Your tools and supplies are scattered everywhere. It looks like 20 percent of your workforce spends all their time looking for tools, supplies, and parts.

"As for JIT, you have 150,000 parts waiting to be assembled. But you only need 800 a day. It will take you 187 days to use up that inventory. That's over nine months. Think about this kitchen. Can you imagine Lesley coming into the dining room and serving us nine months worth of baked potatoes in one sitting?

"I have no doubt that within the one week we will have a very simple, easy to use, JIT parts delivery system working to your satisfaction. It's getting late, I have an early morning tennis game I want to be fresh for. Let's whip out your success plan and call it a night."

They walked back to Bob's office where Bob took out a yellow legal pad and wrote:

Success Plan

1) Brady, issue the "Call to Action"

2) Reduce setup time on the presses

3) Improve assembly process

4) Implement a JIT parts delivery system

5) Improve the maintenance in the press department

Larry read the paper and told Bob, "I agree with everything on this sheet but I think it will take a year to implement all that." Bob stood up, tore the yellow sheet off the pad, placed it into Larry's hand and gently led him toward the front door. "Larry, I've got to get to bed, but I'm confident that we can get all those projects well under way in one week."

> *Do what you can with what you have, where you are.*
>
> T. Roosevelt

Discussion—From a LEAN management standpoint: What's going on in this chapter?

Using a consultant to help with the Lean transformation could be a good idea. There are all kinds of consultants out there. Which brings to mind an old joke.

A shepherd was tending his flock in a remote pasture when suddenly a brand-new Jeep Cherokee appeared out of a dust cloud, advanced toward him and stopped. The driver, a 24-year-old young man wearing a Brioni suit, Gucci shoes, Ray Ban sunglasses and a YSL tie, leaned out of the window and asked our shepherd, "If I can tell you exactly how many sheep you have in your flock, will you give me one?"

The shepherd looked at the young guy, then at his peacefully grazing flock, and calmly answered, "Sure." The young man parked his car, whipped out his notebook computer, connected it to a cell phone, surfed to a NASA page on the Internet where he called up a GPS satellite navigation system, scanned the area, then opened up a database and some Excel spreadsheets with complex formulas. He finally printed out a 150-page report on his hi-tech, miniaturized printer, turned around to our shepherd and said, "You have here exactly 1,586 sheep!"

"Amazing! That's correct! Like I agreed, you can take one of my sheep," said the shepherd.

The shepherd watched the man make a selection and bundle it into his Cherokee. When he was finished the shepherd said, "If I can tell you exactly what you do for a living will you give me my sheep back?"

"Okay, why not," answered the young man.

"You're a management consultant," said the shepherd.

"Wow! That's correct," said the young man. "How did you ever guess that?"

"Easy," answered the shepherd. "You knew you had no experience in my business, but you showed up here anyway. You want to be paid for providing a solution to a question for which I already knew the answer. And, you don't have any idea what you're doing because you just took my dog."

I have nothing against the use of an outside consultants or *sensei* for two reasons. First, an experienced consultant has been through many Lean implementations before and, therefore, owns a "template" to support a smooth implementation. And second, most manufacturing managers become "factory blind." That is, the waste that they walk past every day now looks *normal.* It won't look normal to an outsider.

CHAPTER 9

THE EXPERTS

The consulting firm called SDI, also known as The Synchronized Demand Institute, started their meeting at 8:00 AM Monday morning with Jim Brady. The week before, they had completed their assessment of Sonic and were making their formal presentation that was formatted in a very impressive three-ring binder with sections separated with colored tabs. These were the same three people from SDI who were there the prior week. Frank Farrell, the senior man looked more like a banker than someone familiar with factories. He wore an expensive suit, a monogrammed shirt with gold cufflinks, a gold Rolex and entered the office carrying an $800 Coach brand leather briefcase. His two associates looked to be in their early thirties and were dressed casually—no ties.

Farrell had a booming voice and addressed Jim who was sitting just across his conference table as if he were fifty feet away. Farrell began his presentation with, "Jim I have some bad news and I have some very good news for you. The bad news is that after my two associates spent a week gathering and then analyzing data, we have concluded that your plant here is in a downwards spiral and will probably not last more than eighteen months. The good news is that SDI can turn your situation around very quickly."

Farrell went through his 3-ring binder in great detail. SDI had some ratios that Brady had never seen before and wished he had thought of them himself. The SDI report concluded that the answer to Sonics problem was that SDI be hired to do a number of things, starting with an immediate search for the replacement of Larry Smith.

As Farrell explained, "Your man Smith is a very nice man but unfortunately we don't think he can bring this facility to where it needs to be." Part of our consulting service is a management recruiting agency specializing in operations management. We can put somebody in place that can do the job."

Farrell went on to explain that the disease Sonic was suffering from was their production control system and that implementing a Synchronized Demand system was the cure.

SDI offered a package that included replacing Larry Smith, implementing SDI software, and a conveyorized material delivery system. All this for a fee of $800,000 and an eighteen-month timetable.

Brady was very impressed with Farrell, with SDI, and with their proposed solutions.

> *Tell me I will forget.*
> *Show me I may remember.*
> *Involve me I will understand.*
>
> Chinese Proverb

CHAPTER 10

THE NEWS

Larry was in the machine shop when he saw Jim Brady's secretary, Mary, coming out of the office and heading toward him "Larry, you have to go see Mr. Brady; he needs to speak with you." Larry looked disgusted and shot back, "What does that jerk want from me?" At that point he wished he could make time go backward, retract the words and somehow stuff them back into his mouth. Mary smiled, looked Larry in the face and said, "That's okay, Larry; this guy is the worst boss I've ever had. He knows he's in over his head and has become a monster. I've started looking for another job."

Larry entered Brady's office. Brady was absorbed with his computer where he was busily constructing yet a new chart. Larry patiently sat at Brady's conference table and waited. He marveled once again at the incredible number of charts on his wall. Larry had once read an article about metrics that suggested a company didn't need more than eleven key metrics. Brady must have had one hundred on that wall. The article illustrated the point with a metaphor about a car's dashboard. A car manufacturer could put hundreds of instruments on a dashboard. You could have gages for such things as manifold pressure, exhaust temperature, and exhaust oxygen content. But you actually only need to know five or six key measures and that's what the car manufacturers give you. Any more information than that would obscure the information you really need to pay attention to. The same goes for a factory. There's a danger in too many metrics.

"Hey, how's it going Larry?" Jim finally asked after looking up from his computer. Jim then stood up next to Larry and put his hand on Larry's shoulder. From the day Larry started working for Brady, he noticed that Brady had an annoying habit of putting his hand on the shoulder of the person he was speaking to. Larry thought that Jim thought the gesture was a sign of camaraderie but it was clear that Brady was giving one of those non-verbal signals. This signal said, '*you* work for *me*'—I can touch you whenever I want to, but you better never touch me."

Brady sat down next to Larry and began. "Listen, Larry, I know I've been tough on you. I know you've been giving the job one hundred percent. But irregardless..."

Larry thought, there's that word again, *irregardless* that's not even a word in the English language, I hate this guy. Larry had an urge to get up and punch Brady in the face.

Brady continued, "The numbers simply aren't happening. I just had a meeting with SDI and I'm going to ask Turner to fund their fee. It's almost a million dollars but I think they have the answer to our problems. One of their proposals is to replace you with a candidate familiar with SDI production scheduling software. I'm telling you this because I really don't want you to leave. I plan to make room for you in the organization, but you'll be reporting to the new man."

Larry felt sick. He wanted to lash out, he wanted to stand up and scream, but he decided to not give Brady the satisfaction of having elicited any emotion. So Larry just stared blankly back at Brady.

Brady went on, "I decided that you will help me recruit your new boss. I would like you to interview each candidate and give me your feedback that I promise I will consider."

*Whatever you can do or dream you can
– begin it.
Boldness has genius, power and magic in it.*

Goethe

CHAPTER 11

THE RESCUE

Larry left Brady's office feeling thoroughly defeated. He returned to his office, shut his door, and dialed Bob Simms at his office at Apache. He explained the situation to Simms, who quickly responded, "Larry, let me come out there and speak with Brady. I think I can convince him to let me give him a week of free consulting service. You have nothing to lose at this point, do you?"

"How can you afford to give us one week of consulting service? Nobody works for free."

"I'll tell you why. As I told you before, I have the time. I negotiated three weeks of vacation when Apache recruited me. We're going to Hawaii for a two-week family getaway later in the year. I consider that my holiday. The third week is for me to do something I enjoy and Kaizen is a passion of mine. I'm doing it to help you because you're my friend. And I'm doing it to help my country. I truly believe we need a manufacturing revolution in the United States. Companies with excess capacity in the States are shutting down to get products from abroad. They are giving up without a fight and I want to fight. It's like a revolution and I want to take a leadership role in it."

CHAPTER 11

Larry returned to Brady's office and described his friend, Bob Simms. Larry convinced a reluctant Brady to have a meeting with Simms.

Simms agreed to meet with Brady after hours. That evening, Bob entered Brady's office and was immediately struck by the unusual office: the plethora of charts, the pretentious ornately framed family portrait, and his college degrees.

Brady looked ragged. His pants and shirt looked wrinkled. He had one shirttail half hanging out. Brady began, "Larry speaks very highly of you. I heard a lot about the improvements at Apache Corporation and was anxious to meet the guy responsible for those improvements. I'll admit that the situation here at Sonic is overwhelming, but I think I've found the answer with these consultants at SDI."

The contrast between two people could not have been greater. Brady looked liked he was wearing clothes that had previously been pre-worn by a restless gorilla. Simms looked like he was ready to be photographed for *Gentlemen's Quarterly.*

Simms was his usual calm. He leaned back in the office chair. "Jim, I think I can help you. Let me ask you five questions. Maybe this will give you a new perspective to your problems here. For the moment, forget about the current difficulties you're having with bottlenecks and quality. Let's try looking at this from 50,000 feet. Your current problems aren't really problems at all—they're symptoms. Let me help you pinpoint your underlying problems that led to today's mess.

Simms listed the five questions. He began, "First question—How will you grow your business? Second question—Where will this growth come from? From which customers? Third question—What needs do these customers have that you need to resolve? Fourth question—Who ARE your competitors? Fifth question—How will you compete to win?"

Brady sat there stunned. "You're blowing me away with these questions. You are right, I am totally focused on the symptoms and I have given very little thought to the issues you raise. I can answer all five questions in general terms. I know the names of my competition but know nothing whatsoever about their capabilities. I cannot cope with my company's growth. My customers all hate me. They don't mind my prices but are very unhappy with my delivery and quality."

"Listen, Brady, I think I can help you. Larry Smith is a good friend of mine and I think I have a plan that could help your company and bail out my friend Larry. Right now your company is bleeding and we have to stop that bleeding. A prolonged study to gather data is the last thing you need right now. Right now you need action.

"One of my skills is leading Kaizen events. It's a way of improving processes very quickly by focusing on the elimination of waste in those processes. I propose we take your most screwed up department and fix it. It will take one week and the improved department we create will serve as a model for the rest of your plant. I urge you to do this because you have nothing to lose, I won't charge you a cent and you'll be using your own people—not some high-priced consultants. I will train your people during that week. At the end of the week, you will not only have improved your worst performing department, you will also remove a constraint and you will have a dozen of your own people fully trained in an effective, proven method of bringing about dramatic improvement quickly."

Brady leaned forward and stared at Simms. "I must admit—your offer is tempting. I've read books on Kaizen, on 5S, on the SMED method of setup time reduction, on constraint elimination. While the books were all interesting, none of them took me step-by-step through the implementation. I've read in the local paper about the impressive improvements over at Apache. I need help and at this point I'm ready to try anything. But tell me, how do we decide which department to do this Kaizen event in?"

Simms replied, "The project we pick is important. We now have two clues as to which department to pick. The first clue can be seen in the Manufacturing Quick Survey that Larry and I completed. Ask him to give you a copy. That survey showed that one of the biggest failures in your factory is the lack of flow. Each department is producing at a pace independent of the department it is feeding. Each department is just pushing and piling inventory into the next. What you have to aim for in transforming this place is the *radical* almost un-imaginable idea of a synchronized flow of all material throughout the value stream, without buffers.

"The second clue to picking a project will be from the value stream maps we created. The value stream maps illuminate those areas that potentially could serve as targets for the event. Selecting the first target is crucial since this will be the organization's *pilot* introduction to Kaizen and you want to start with a winner. This pilot project will not only demonstrate the potential of lean manufacturing, it will also be the breeding ground for a team of skilled implementers. After the pilot ends, the team is disbanded and the members propagate the skills and knowledge they just acquired."

Simms walked over to Brady's chalkboard. "I'm going to write criteria and leave them on your board for you and your people to contemplate for the next few days. It will help you select a department to start in. I would make this choice carefully—your first Kaizen event has to be a winner."

Bob wrote three sentences on the chalkboard:

1) *Is the process dysfunctional?*

2) *Will the customer benefit if the process were improved?*

3) *Is there a high likelihood that a Kaizen event will improve the process?*

Bob explained what he had written. "The department we pick has to satisfy these three conditions. But in addition to the three criteria above, there are other considerations in selecting this first Kaizen event. First of all, the project has to be justifiable by putting it into financial terms. This does two things: it justifies the project but it also gets the financial people involved up front. There are three other considerations to think about. I'll write these down as well for you."

Bob added three more phrases:

4) *Is the importance of the project clear to the entire organization?*

5) *Does the project have clear quantifiable measures of success?*

6) *Does the project have the support of upper management so that they can approve resources and remove obvious barriers?*

Brady studied the writing and concluded, "I've been studying the situation in the shop for weeks. It's obvious that the place to focus on is final assembly. The place is a mess. I've tried to explain that to your buddy Smith, but he won't listen."

Simms was still standing next to the chalkboard. "Do me a favor. Don't be hasty in picking the process tonight. Discuss it with your people. Please use these six points to help you. Engage your staff. You'll be glad you did.

Brady looked irritated. "You're speaking to me as if I decided to let you come work with us. I've spent a lot of time with the SDI people and still think they can help me."

Simms calmly replied "Think about my offer. I can be here next week from Monday through Friday and I'm confident I can make a big difference to you."

Brady asked, "I'm a bit confused. What exactly is Lean Manufacturing and what does that have to do with Kaizen?"

"I love that question," replied Simms. "There are countless definitions of 'Lean.' Rather than wrestle with definitions, it is more useful to examine the metrics that show proof that there is progress toward Lean. These metrics typically include:

♦ Increased throughput and capacity

♦ Reduced lead times

♦ More floor space available for production

♦ Greater gross margin

♦ Higher inventory turns (raw, WIP, finished goods)

♦ Improved workplace organization

♦ Improved employee morale and participation

There is confusion about how the concepts of Lean and Kaizen relate to one another. Kaizen is a Japanese word meaning "continuous improvement." It describes a technique that has proven to bring about improvements in productivity and quality. The process-driven tools under the Kaizen umbrella include TPM, SMED, Kanban, One-Piece-Flow, Continuous Flow and JIT. Clearly, successful application of these specific tools will improve each of the Lean performances I just mentioned.

"Kaizen is a method of continuous *incremental* improvement. Toyota developed an approach called Kaikaku that means 'radical improvement.' In the West we don't typically use the word, Kaikaku. We have westernized the term into *Kaizen Event, Kaizen Blitz, Breakthrough Kaizen, Flow Kaizen, and Systems Kaizen.* The Kaizen Blitz has been used successfully as a key Lean implementation tool to bring about dramatic improvements in productivity and quality *within one week*. You were ready to pay hundreds of thousands of dollars to a consulting company. The Kaizen Blitz typically does not result in spending money for capital—there simply isn't time.

"Let me offer you some additional advice. If you're really interested in kicking off a Kaizen event, what you're really doing is kicking off a 'Lean Transformation.' One of the key activities of the Lean transformation is the 'Call to Action.' This requires that you, Jim, the chief executive, assemble every employee and explain that the company cannot continue doing business as it has in the past, that if the business is to survive, they have to do business differently and that means everyone will have to change—change fast. That means *everyone.*

"The call to action is vital in overcoming organizational inertia, flushing out cultural barriers to change, and making it clear that the transformation must be enterprise-wide. *Everyone* must change. This message will do two things: it will make it clear that you are 100% behind the initiative and that this is a serious project for the whole company.

"Besides picking the right process to improve, one of the other keys to the success of the Kaizen event is the effectiveness with which *a sense of crisis* is created. An important ingredient in the weeklong event is that the team feels a very strong sense of urgency. This is achieved by the formulation of the goals the team is given.

"Typical goals to be achieved in five days could be, for example, such things as to double output per person or to cut the floor space used by fifty percent. The team is typically stunned by the enormity of the task and may even feel it to be impossible. This creates a high degree of teamwork and a focusing of the collective minds."

Simms concluded, "Think over what I've said and give me a call tomorrow if you really want to go through with this. I'm sure you can hold off on hiring those consultants since no money has yet changed hands. I'm offering you an opportunity to not only save your company but also to solidify a relationship with your staff that is sorely missing."

Brady stood up and approached Simms. "Look Bob, you're a nice guy, you seem to know what you're talking about. My job is on the line here. I have confidence in the SDI people. I don't know anything about you."

Bob just stared at Brady as he developed an

argument. "Okay, Jim, I can accept that. Let me make you an offer. Come visit me at Apache and see with your own eyes what our Lean transformation looks like. All I ask is that you hold off your decision until after you visit Apache."

Simms left Brady in his office and drove to Larry Smith's house. He rang the bell and Sue answered the door. Bob could see from the doorway that Larry was at the kitchen table helping little Tommy with homework. Simms told Larry what had happened that evening at Brady's office. Larry asked, "Do you really think Brady will go for this?"

> *The girl who can't dance*
> *says the band can't play.*
>
> Yiddish Proverb

- Focusing on Syptoms & Not The Problems.
- Synchronized Flow Throughout The Value Stream.

CHAPTER 12

THE TOUR

Jim Brady decided to visit Apache. He was impressed immediately with the front lobby. He was surprised to see all the activity going on there. There were Apache employees speaking with one another as well as Apache employees talking to visitors. The thing Brady noticed was that the Apache people all seemed to be in great moods. They seemed to be having a good time. He had to admit to himself that the typical Sonic employee usually looked stressed, angry, or just sad.

Brady had to wait in the lobby only for about five minutes when Simms came bounding in. Simms was smiling and quickly made his way across to Brady and shook his hand vigorously. "Jim, I'm so happy you decided to visit Apache. I think you'll find the time well spent."

As they left the lobby through the door leading to the factory, the first thing that struck Brady was how bright the lighting level made the place look. The walls looked freshly painted and the aisles were marked and clear of clutter. Brady was constantly frustrated with Sonic's aisles that were always in a mess with raw material and work-in-process.

As soon as Brady and Simms began walking in the factory, people would look up and give a friendly wave and smile to Simms. Simms and Brady couldn't walk fifty feet without an Apache employee approaching Simms either to give him information or just a friendly hello. Yet another contrast with Sonic, thought Brady. Brady had to admit that when people in his factory saw him coming, they often would walk the other way or just keep their heads down to avoid any conversation.

Brady couldn't help notice the *pace* of the operation. People were doing their assembly and fabrication jobs quickly, and he was surprised at how quickly people were walking. There seemed to be a sense of urgency about the place, yet nobody looked stressed. People were smiling and looked as if they were enjoying themselves.

Brady noticed how similar the processes were between Sonic and Apache. Both factories were well vertically integrated with extensive fabrication as well as assembly operations. But the differences were profound. Sonic looked more like a warehouse than a factory. Materials were stored throughout the factory on twelve-foot-high shelving, making it impossible to see anything going on. The Apache factory had nothing in it over four and one-half feet high. There was very little material visible and you could see the entire factory from any position on the floor.

Brady began reflecting on what he would normally observe people doing at Sonic compared with Apache. At Apache, everyone was at their workstations or walking quickly on their way to someplace. At Sonic, there were many people who appeared to be looking for things. They were looking for materials, for tools, for paperwork. Or maybe they were at their workstations and idle because of material shortages, mechanical breakdowns, or bottlenecks.

It looked like all the materials at Apache were within reach of the operators. At Sonic, most of the operators had to walk to get their own materials and bring them to their workstations.

After about ten minutes of Simms leading Brady, he stopped and said, "So, Jim, what do you think so far?" Brady thought for a second and replied, "I am very impressed. I visited this plant some time ago—before you started here. The place was a mess. Many of our employees at Sonic came from Apache. They left because they hated working there. Management was weak, working conditions were uncomfortable and often just plain dangerous. I can't believe the transformation in such little time. Apache was in much worse condition than Sonic is now."

Bob Simms was beaming at this point. "Jim, I think I'll have you meet one of our lead operators on an assembly line and have her tell you about Apache from an employees perspective."

Simms and Brady walked into the assembly department and approached a woman standing next to the assembly line and holding a stopwatch that was attached to a lanyard around her neck.

She smiled as soon as she saw Simms approaching. "Hi, Bob, how's it going?"

"Hi, Carla. I'd like you to meet Jim Brady. Would you mind showing him your assembly line?"

Carla shook hands with Brady and then led him to a bulletin board adjacent to the assembly line. "This bulletin board pretty much tells the story. Each section of the factory has it's own bulletin board to control it's operation. This chart here is what I'm most concerned with."

She pointed to a piece of paper on the bulletin board that was the size of two 8½ x 11- inch sheets. There was a kind of chart on it that looked very much like the scoreboard of a baseball game. Instead of being divided into nine innings, it was divided into eight hours of the workday. The chart was used to give an hourly target for each hour of work and then to record how they performed against the target each hour.

Carla explained, "My number one job is to make sure that we hit each hourly target. Our Takt Time is sixty seconds per unit so we are expected to produce sixty units per hour. Of course, in those hours that we take our breaks for coffee or lunch, the goal is less than sixty units."

Brady was impressed. A few days ago he had no idea what Takt Time was and here's an hourly operator expert in its application.

Carla led Brady on a walk down the assembly line. "What we have here, Mr. Brady, is a progressive assembly line. The idea is that all operators do the exact amount of work so that there is a smooth flow and no bottlenecks. My main job is to maintain that flow. I use my stopwatch to make sure that operators on the assembly line spend the same number of seconds to complete their element of work. When there is an imbalance, I redistribute the tasks. I rebalance the line. So far today we are hitting our Takt Time and we will meet the production schedule."

Carla smiled, "I was on the original Kaizen team that set this line up. It only took a week and we got the line to produce fifty percent more with one-third fewer operators. We used to rework about ten percent of what this line produced. We now have less than one percent rework."

Brady was impressed. Very impressed. He couldn't think of one part of the Sonic factory that worked as efficiently as this assembly line. "Tell me, Carla," he asked, "What are those other papers on your bulletin board?"

They walked back to the board where Carla pointed to a paper showing the schedule for the week and how they were performing so far against it. The other papers dealt with projects the Kaizen team was working on. There were tables showing types of defects and what actions were in progress to address them. One page had a list of ongoing projects to improve output.

What struck Brady was that each action had a due date and a person assigned to it. As his eyes scanned the factory, he saw that there were dozens of these bulletin boards. The entire facility was being controlled on an hourly basis against Takt Times and there were hundreds of projects listed to make even more improvements.

"Tell me, Carla," Brady asked, "Do you ever run out of materials?" Carla's eyes lit up. "Before Kaizen, we were constantly running out of materials—not only purchased parts but parts made in our own fabrication departments. It was our biggest problem. At first we would solve the part shortage problem by switching the line over to produce a product that we did have the parts for. That turned into a disaster. We loaded our warehouse with products nobody wanted. After that, we just would send people home when their department had a parts shortage."

Simms joined Carla and Brady at the bulletin board. "Thank you, Carla; we better let you get back to work. Come on Jim, I'll buy you a cup of coffee in the break room."

On the way to the break room, Simms took Brady on a tour of the fabrication departments. He was stunned with the cleanliness and obvious smooth running order of what at Sonic would be a sloppy group of departments.

"I took you to Carla's assembly line for a reason. That was where we conducted our first Kaizen event and it was a winner. That pilot project kicked off our Lean transformation. The second Kaizen project was to solve our material shortages by implementing a plant-wide material pull system using Kanbans. That not only solved our shortage problem but had a dramatic effect on our inventory turns. After that, we turned our attention to the fabrication departments. Our problems there were long setup times, a lot of scrap, and very long lead times. Those problems are all behind us now."

Brady had finished his cup of coffee and was now staring into the empty cup. He looked up at Simms. "I'm blown away with what I've seen here this morning. I have a lot of thinking to do. I also have to discuss this with my boss, Ed Turner. He has approved going ahead with the consulting contract and now I need to tell him about you. Give me until tomorrow to get back to you."

Nothing in the world
can take the place of persistence.

TALENT will not; nothing is more common
than unsuccessful people with TALENT.

GENIUS will not; unrewarded GENIUS is
almost a proverb.

EDUCATION will not; the world is full of
EDUCATED derelicts.

PERSISTENCE and DETERMINATION alone
are omnipotent.

Ray Kroc, McDonald's Restaurants

CHAPTER 13

GETTING READY

Brady called Simms the next morning, giving him the go-ahead. Simms immediately called Larry Smith to give him the good news.

"Brady called me a few minutes ago and approved my coming in to work at Sonic for a week and I believe he will take a leadership role. Brady will kick off the event but he will be relying on you to manage it. Tomorrow I believe he will assemble his staff to select a target process to improve and shortly after that he will be making the big announcement. But it will be up to you to manage this and your first task will be to assemble a team.

"The two considerations in team formation are size and skill requirements. The ideal team size is six to ten people. If the group is larger than ten, I recommend they get broken into two teams—each given separate goals to achieve. Teams with more than ten people are difficult to manage and tend to interfere with one another.

"The composition of the team is critical. If the team consisted only of technical and management personnel, it would lack the vital contribution from the factory personnel. But without team members from the factory, it would be difficult to make the process changes 'stick' very long. On the other hand, if the team consisted only of factory personnel, two problems would occur. First, the team would lack technical and logistical information and skills as well as the resources that members of management could call upon for help. And second, a great deal of the time during the week is spent gathering data. Much of this data is in the form of time studies of people working on the processes that need improving. If everyone were assigned to gathering data, there would be nobody left to study. The team, therefore, must be a mix of factory personnel and support staff. Ideally, some members of the team should come from areas away from the area being studied. Those people tend to ask the best questions. The support people needn't be technical—office staffs are often fascinated to learn about their factory."

Bob continued to explain the event: "Let's take the example of a Kaizen event that will focus on improving a fabrication department manned by 12 people. The team could consist of:

√ 3 Assemblers from that line

√ 1 Industrial Engineer or Manufacturing Engineer

√ 1 person from the Materials organization

√ 1 Maintenance technician

√ 1 Office worker (accounting, purchasing, development engineering, marketing)

"We need to think about leadership and team

facilitation. The leader of the Kaizen team does not necessarily have to be the normal leader of the production personnel. A manufacturing engineer or lead operator with good leadership skills could work out well. It is critical, however, that the person assigned to lead the Kaizen team be held accountable for the *continued* success of the improvement efforts."

Larry suggested that the fabrication supervisor would be a good candidate for leading the team. Greg Timbers was twenty-five years old. He started with the company right out of high school and was taking evening courses in industrial engineering.

Bob said that team facilitation would be his role. His job would be vital to maintain momentum during the week's event. He would be conducting the event, keeping the team on track, anticipating and removing roadblocks, keeping upper management appraised of progress throughout the week, and assisting with the preparation of the final presentation to top management. Larry Smith will play a vital role in following up after the completion of the week's activities.

Bob continued, "We have to talk about the kick-off. I need you to tell your staff that next week we will be conducting Kaizen events in the shop and we need them to spread the word. We need everyone in the company to know that we will be doing a Lean implementation and the need for it. They have also heard that a Kaizen Event is imminent where dramatic improvements will take place but they are assured that these types of activities will not result in wholesale staff reduction. The six to ten people selected to work for one week on the Kaizen event must be notified in writing that they have been selected for this very important assignment. The letter will describe the area that the team will be assigned to but the letter must NOT reveal the goals. It's important that the goals come as a surprise (or maybe a shock) to the team when they are first assembled.

"The letter they receive should explain that their selection should be considered a privilege, not a punishment. It must explain that the week they spend on Kaizen is a full-time effort. They will not be pulled away from the team to attend meetings or to return to their normal jobs at any time during the week. Also, they must understand that some of the days during the Kaizen Event will be quite long and they might have to make personal arrangements to accommodate extended days.

"Larry, if we're going to be spending next week doing Kaizen, I need to go back to the factory and look around some more. Can I come by after work tomorrow? I would like to look at the fabrication areas and the assembly lines."

The next day Larry was called into Brady's office first thing. This time Brady was not at his computer and was not looking at his wall of charts. He was just sitting at his desk. "Look Larry," Brady began, "by now you know I had a meeting with Simms the other night and he offered to spend next week giving us free consulting advice and conducting Kaizen events. I wasn't convinced by what he had to say. Seemed like a know-it-all. But he had me visit Apache and he persuaded me that he really knows what he's doing. I'm at the point where I'm willing to try anything. I'm going to hold an "all hands meeting" this afternoon to announce that things around here have to get better and in order for that to happen things have got to change. That means all of us have to change and change fast—starting with ME.

"I'm going to announce that we are going to become a Lean company and that transition will begin next week with Kaizen. I need you to pick a team or maybe teams and I expect you to take a leadership role with that and the follow up. Simms asked me to compose a letter to the teams. I need your advice for those goals."

Larry responded, "I'm meeting Simms here this evening and we'll come up with those goals then."

That day was spent with Brady preparing for and then delivering his speech to the company. He made a PowerPoint presentation showing in very clear terms how far the company had fallen from their prior performance levels. The audience was shocked by the condition of the company but was reassured by his explanation that the problems were all about to be aggressively tackled and that there were no plans to reduce staff.

Larry overheard two of the factory operators after Brady's speech. "Here we go again—more BOHICA" said one old timer. "Bohica?" asked the second operator. "That's right Bohica. Haven't you ever heard of it? It stands for Bend Over, Here It Comes Again!"

That evening Simms visited the plant and took a tour with Larry Smith and Greg Timbers. The Value Stream Map was their guide. They concentrated on the press area and the assembly lines. Greg was immediately defensive and told Simms that there was no reason to focus on the stamping presses since his charts showed the area to be 85% efficient and setups were no problem at all.

Simms responded, "Let me ask you two questions, Greg. First, tell me how long it takes to convert a flat piece of raw sheet steel into the final product in a shipping carton. And second, tell me how many minutes of actual 'touch time' that represents."

Timbers scratched his head and rolled his eyeballs up as if the answers were written on the top of his eye sockets, "I worked on that charting exercise with Larry and I recall that the time from raw sheet steel to finished product was about three weeks. Three weeks is during normal times. Right now we have so many shortages that it's taking months to move a part through our system. As for the touch time, I would estimate that to less than an hour."

"That sounds about right," said Simms. "Now can you tell me how on earth something that takes less than sixty minutes to make has to spend three weeks or more sitting in the factory? What this plant needs is *velocity*. The quicker we can make the product, the better will be the customer service and your cash flow. The ideal model is McDonald's—they get your money for that hamburger BEFORE they have to pay for the meat.

There are companies in the US that have achieved a manufacturing velocity that allows them to receive payment for their product BEFORE they have to pay for their raw materials. That means they have achieved *negative working capital.*"

"How long does it take to set up a typical die set?" Bob asked. "Typically it takes forty-five minutes," estimated Greg.

"I think we can have one team here focusing on reducing your setup times to under ten minutes."

"That's impossible," Greg retorted. "If we have a rush job we can do a setup in about twenty-five minutes. I'll tell you right now that ten minutes is impossible. As a matter of fact, I'll bet you a beer that ten minutes is impossible."

Simms had them move into the assembly area. "This simply does not look like a factory to me. It's more like a warehouse. A well-designed factory shouldn't have anything higher than four feet in it, allowing everyone to see what's going on. Everything is surrounded with ten-foot racks packed with stock. Operations aren't adjacent to one another. There are long material travel distances and long people travel distances. This place is ripe for our picking. We need a second team to implement one-piece flow in your assembly area and create a logical, simplified, material delivery system."

The next morning Greg came into Larry's office holding a memo. "I guess Brady is serious. About twenty-five people received this memo today. It's Brady's announcement of our kick-off."

"I got my copy today," replied Larry holding up his copy.

Dear Fellow Employee,

As you know we are embarking on a journey to become a LEAN company. The first step will be a series of Kaizen events. You have been selected to participate in an event next week. The event will kick off 7:30 Monday morning and continue until the end of the workday on Friday.

This will be a full time effort for you. That means you will not be attending any other meetings or answering any telephone or email messages for one week during normal working hours.

Jim Brady
General Manager

Jim Brady walked into Larry's office and slumped into one of the guest chairs. "Well, I've committed myself to Lean, to Kaizen and to your friend Bob Simms. I've sent out twenty-five copies of the letter and I'm ready to personally kick the events off next Monday morning. I believe we will have two teams with eight members each. That's sixteen people doing Kaizen. But Simms plans to spend the first day explaining Lean manufacturing and Kaizen. He asked me to have eight of our key people attend that first day. These will be eight people not participating in Kaizen. I will have my five direct reports plus three shop managers of your choosing. The more people that buy into this, the better it will work.

"I need your input of the exact goals for the two Kaizen teams so that I can put those into a letter to be handed out Monday at 7:30 AM when Simms gets here."

> *Trust men and they will be true to you. Treat them greatly and they will show themselves great.*
>
> R.W. Emerson

Lean Implementation Steps

√ Business assessment

√ Call to action

√ Training and/or *SENSEI*

√ Create LEAN promotion function

√ Value stream mapping

√ Begin Kaizen events

√ Implement new metrics

√ Expand LEAN disciplines

Typical Order of Steps Taken in Implementing an Enterprise-Wide Lean Implementation.

CHAPTER 14

THE FUTURE STATE

Larry pulled into his driveway after work on Friday night. He looked into his living room picture window and could see Bob and Lesley Simms were in there with Sue and had already broken out the beer.

He opened the front door and announced, "Hi, Lucy, I'm home!"

"Come on back here," Bob called back. "Grab yourself a brew."

Larry sat down heavily in his lounge chair and savored his cold beer. "I can't wait for next week. I really believe we're going to turn this mess around with you leading the charge, Bob."

"So, Larry, are you ready for a rematch on the tennis court tomorrow?"

Larry closed his eyes and pictured his last humbling defeat by Bob. "I don't think my ego can endure much more punishment. What I would like to do is spend tonight with you and Lesley at the pizza joint in town and then spend Saturday doing some more preparation for next week."

"You're right, Larry, we do have a lot to get done before Monday. Let's have fun tonight and dedicate Saturday to preparation."

Larry was at Bob's house first thing Saturday morning. Larry, unshaven, was wearing his faded gardening jeans. The edges of the pockets and knees were almost white from wear. He had on an old tee shirt with green paint stains on the front. Simms' jeans had knife-sharp creases ironed in. He wore a golf shirt with the logo of the local country club on the breast. He was clean-shaven and looked his usual meticulous, relaxed self.

Bob took out some papers to show Larry. "Look here, Larry. I've been doing some preparation on my own. I've completed three little charts. The first one shows the current state as compared to the future state value stream map. I want you to see how dramatic the improvements are going to be. We will be able to improve the velocity of the shop from three months down to three days. Not only that, but we can drop the inventory levels from 540,000 to 37,000 units.

"We have to launch an attack in three separate areas: shearing, stamping, and assembly. Next week we can focus on Kaizen events in stamping and assembly; the shearing department will have to wait a few weeks."

Bob and Larry spent the rest of the day organizing their data and selecting members of the two teams.

*The jawbone of an ass
is just as dangerous a weapon today
as it was in Samson's time.*

Anon

THE CURRENT STATE

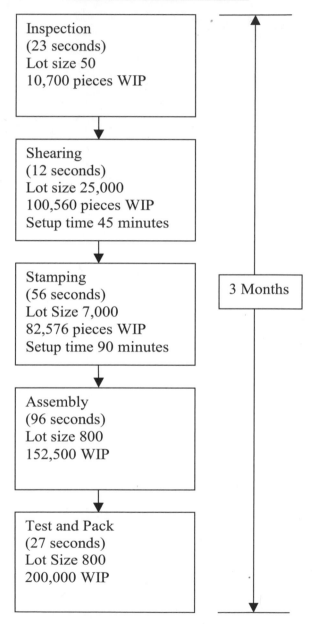

THE FUTURE STATE

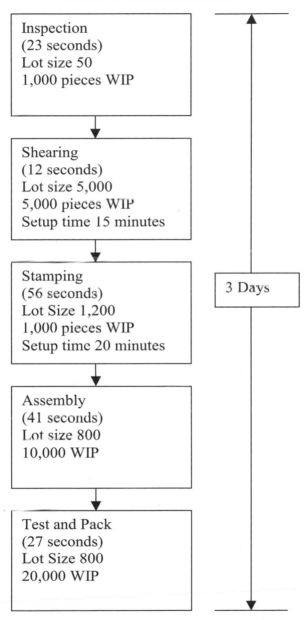

Inspection
(23 seconds)
Lot size 50
1,000 pieces WIP

Shearing
(12 seconds)
Lot size 5,000
5,000 pieces WIP
Setup time 15 minutes

Stamping
(56 seconds)
Lot Size 1,200
1,000 pieces WIP
Setup time 20 minutes

Assembly
(41 seconds)
Lot size 800
10,000 WIP

Test and Pack
(27 seconds)
Lot Size 800
20,000 WIP

3 Days

Operation	Velocity		Inventory (Pcs)	
	Current	Future	Current	Future
Inspection	3 Days	1 Day	10,000	1,000
Shearing	5 Days	1/2 Day	100,000	5,000
Stamping	2 Days	1/2 Day	80,000	1,000
Assembly	6 Days	1/2 Day	150,000	10,000
Test and Pack	3 Days	1/2 Day	200,000	20,000
Total	19 Days	3 Days	540,000	37,000

Area	Shear	Stamp	Assembly
Strategy	Improve Maintenance	Reduce Setup Times	One-piece flow and improved material delivery system
Benefit	Eliminate buffer stock	Reduce lot size	Increase pieces per person per day

These are the three charts Bob showed to Larry. The first one compares the current state to the future state. The second summarizes the improvements to manufacturing velocity and inventory levels. The third shows the strategies and

benefits to the three target areas: shearing, stamping, and assembly.

CHAPTER 15

THE KICKOFF

Monday morning at 7:30 AM the conference room was full. At the front of the room were Jim Brady, Bob Simms, and Larry Smith. The tables and chairs were arranged classroom style. Jim Brady's direct reports were there along with the three production supervisors, an industrial engineer, the head of maintenance, a buyer, and fifteen shop floor personnel.

There was a coffee urn in the back of the room with several boxes of donuts. Across the front of the room were a TV with built-in VCR, two flipcharts, an overhead projector, and a screen for both the overhead projector and a digital projector attached to a laptop.

Brady stood up. "Good morning everyone. Each of you received a letter from me inviting you to this weeklong event. I want to remind you that this isn't punishment. You should be flattered to have been selected. Our conversion to Lean manufacturing is very important to me. You will have my complete support this coming week for whatever you may need. This group is divided into two parts. Sixteen of you will be assigned to teams to do Kaizen in the stamping and assembly areas. You will spend all week on these projects. Eight of you will be here only for the first day that will be a lecture on Lean manufacturing and Kaizen.

"You've heard me say this before and now you'll hear me say it again, 'We have to change the way we do business if we hope to survive.' I believe that Kaizen will make us more productive. Don't have any fears that increased productivity will result in staff reductions. You have my word that there will be no staff reductions that result from any productivity improving measures. I've never been accused of being 'Mr. Nice Guy' and this isn't an opportunity for that. I'm making this guarantee not to be charitable but to be strategic. I want to do many more Kaizen type events after this one and if this one results in layoffs, that will create fear that will mean that future Kaizen events will not get your full support and ultimately will fail.

"I have outlined my challenge to you. I'll project an image of it onto the screen and also give each of you a copy for yourselves."

Dear Kaizen Team Member:

You have two challenges for the week. I expect these to be achieved by Friday and would appreciate a formal PowerPoint presentation of your success on Friday at 1:00 PM.

Stamping Improvement Team
√ Reduce setup time from an average of 90 minutes to 30 minutes.
√ Reduce WIP inventory by 90%
√ Install a "pull" material delivery system

Assembly Improvement Team
√ Increase pieces per person per day by 25%
√ Reduce floor space used by 25%
√ Install a "pull" material delivery system.

Brady handed out the challenge sheets to all present in the room while they absorbed what was up on the screen. Groans were heard, followed by laughter. "You have got to be kidding Mr. Brady. We were never near these numbers, even when we were at our best," one of the most outspoken of the group offered.

Brady went rigid. What little friendliness shown on his face disappeared and was replaced with a scowl. "No, I'm not kidding and this isn't a joke. I'm convinced that these numbers are attainable and that you are the people who can do it." Brady walked over to where Bob Simms was standing.

"I want you all to meet somebody. This is Bob Simms. He's the general manager of the Apache plant. We all know about the phenomenal growth those Apache people have been enjoying this past year. They were in a lot worse shape than we are in. I know many of you have friends or relatives that work there. Those of you know that those improvements happened after Bob Simms joined them. Bob has agreed to spend one week here and teach us the tools that he employed to bring about their success. I think you will all enjoy working with Bob and I'm sure that by Friday we will all have something to celebrate.

"I'll leave you all with Bob now and see you again in this room on Friday at 1:00 PM. Have fun!"

Simms stood up, wrote his name on the flip chart, and introduced himself in a friendly easy-going style. He told them about his background and his hobbies. He then surprised the group by asking each person in turn to stand up and describe their job as well as what they did for fun after work and on weekends. Bob then walked over to the flip chart.

"If we want to improve these departments to the levels we have been challenged with, obviously things have to change. But we have to change things in a very special way," Bob explained as he wrote on the flipchart.

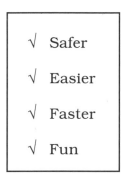

√ Safer

√ Easier

√ Faster

√ Fun

"I've visited your plant several times and I see how hard you all work here. You don't need to work any harder. Whatever changes we come up with this week will have to result in your work becoming safer, faster, easier, and fun. All our efforts will be directed toward these things.

"I'm going to spend the rest of the day lecturing on Lean manufacturing and Kaizen. Then tomorrow morning we will break up into the two teams and begin our projects. Lean and Kaizen are my favorite subjects to talk about and I'm going to try very hard to make this day enjoyable, and interesting and hopefully give you some tools that you can use not only here at work but at home as well."

The people in the room relaxed as soon as Jim Brady left. They were apprehensive about Simms but after listening to him for a few minutes were totally relaxed and ready to give him a chance. At least most of the group was. There were still skeptics—particularly the shop supervisors.

The shop supervisors were all old-timers who worked their way up from the entry-level labor positions. They ruled the shop with iron hands and seemed to have a slogan, "power is knowing."

The first lecture topic Bob presented was on the fundamentals of Kaizen. He explained that the Japanese word *Kaizen* was made up of two Japanese words, *Kai* meaning "Change" and *Zen* meaning "For the better." Taken together, the two words translate into "Continuous Improvement." Kaizen means continuous improvement. Kaizen consists of three principal elements: elimination of waste, good housekeeping, and standardization of processes. He also covered the importance of teamwork and the mandatory establishment of the non-blaming culture. The over-riding concept he conveyed was that changes had to be made in order to bring about improvement and these changes must make work safer, faster, easier, and FUN.

The second topic dealt with waste elimination. The concept he got across was that results could be improved only by improving the process. And processes are improved by the permanent elimination of waste. The Japanese word for *waste* is *Muda*. The challenge is that the Muda is hidden and must be hunted for in a disciplined manner. The discipline required is the breaking down of Muda to the seven categories:

- ◆ Muda of overproduction

- ◆ Muda of conveyance

- ◆ Muda of excess inventory

- ◆ Muda of wasted motion

- Muda of excess processing

- Muda of waiting

- Muda of producing failures

Those lectures lasted until lunchtime. The four hours went very quickly. Bob's audience was fascinated with his lectures. Bob and Larry stayed in the conference room with the group while they ate their catered-in lunch of pizza and salad.

One plant worker, a middle aged woman, said to Bob, "You know something, Bob, "I've been working here at Sonic for twelve years and the attitude toward us workers has always been 'just leave your brains at the door when you get here in the morning —you're not paid to think, just to be told what to do.'"

Another shop worker, a young man in his twenties, piped in, "Mr. Simms, I started here three years ago. When I first got here I thought of lots of ideas for improvement. I told them to my supervisor and to the industrial engineer. In every case, I was either told that they had already tried my idea and it failed or that what I was suggesting wasn't practical. Eventually I just stopped offering any suggestions. They weren't really interested."

That comment from the shop worker struck a chord with Bob. "You were the victim of what's called 'killer phrases.'" Those are that phrases that kill off any hope of new ideas. Other typical phrases include: 'Yes but...', 'We've tried that before,' 'Don't rock the boat,' 'Put it in writing,' 'Let's stick with what works,' I'll get back to you,' 'It isn't your responsibility.'"

Bob was having a good time. It was clear he loved lecturing on the subject and, unlike Jim Brady, he was very comfortable eating and chatting with plant personnel. Bob worked up an appetite doing his lecture. He made the subjects fun, interjecting many stories to illustrate his points along with many very funny jokes just to keep things moving.

Bob put down his third slice of pizza. "You won't have to worry about your ideas being rejected this week, I can promise you that. I don't know the first thing about loudspeaker manufacturing and you are the experts as far as I am concerned. If during this week any of you have an idea that has a 50-50 chance of working, we're going to go for it. If we're wrong, we'll just correct our errors. If I had to come up with a slogan for Kaizen it would have to be something like, 'Just do it and do it NOW.'"

After lunch Bob introduced his next topic, Methods of Standardization. The concept he conveyed was that there can only be *one* way of performing a process and that way must be the safest, fastest, and easiest. He demonstrated his concept with an entertaining game. He organized a contest where the winner was the one who put the most peanuts in a paper cup in sixty seconds using chopsticks, his point being that one method has to be better than all other methods. Each person in the class was given a paper cup, a handful of peanuts, and a pair of chopsticks. They were given one minute to put the peanuts one-at-a-time into the cups. One person only got four peanuts in the cup. He had never used chopsticks before. The winner put sixty peanuts in his cup. Bob had the class all try the winner's method of holding the chopsticks and filling the cup. The results were that the scores improved tremendously and the variability, that is, the range of results was much narrower.

Bob explained that standardization and industrial housekeeping go hand in hand. The Japanese method of creating "a place for everything and everything in its place" is a discipline called 5S. Bob illustrated 5S with commercial videos on the subject and with photographs of successful implementations. 5S, he explained becomes an essential foundation not only for *standardization of work* but for creation of the *visual workplace.*

By mid-afternoon, Bob introduced the concept of flow production. This, he explained, is the most difficult concept to get across. The *radical* idea of a synchronized flow of all material throughout the value stream, without buffers, is almost unimaginable to some. There are many simulation exercises available such as the Lego or paper airplane games. Bob did a simulation exercise with paper airplanes. He organized the class into an assembly line to produce these airplanes. He created a sort of assembly line with each person making just one fold and then passing their work to the next position for the subsequent fold until the airplane was completed, First they tried making the planes in batches of five for a period of ten minutes. Then, they repeated the exercise using one-piece-flow for ten minutes. When the team switched to one-piece-flow their output increase by a factor of ten and they produced 90% less work in process inventory.

When they tried producing in batches, Bob forced them to use a "push" type material delivery system with each person working as fast as they could just piling inventory into the next position. With the one-piece flow, he had each person pull work from the previous folder so that there was zero inventory between positions.

Bob had to be sure that his idea of *Pull vs. Push* was thoroughly understood in order for the training to be meaningful. He felt that Sonic's biggest problem was that their pushing inventory throughout their system was the reason for their lack of flow. During this phase of the training the concepts of Kanban and JIT were introduced.

Since half of this Kaizen event focused on the assembly line, Bob realized that they would be creating one-piece flow on the one assembly line. This would involve creating a balanced line and perhaps creating a U-shaped line. This required the training in the concept of *TAKT* Time and the use of stopwatches to gather accurate data on Takt Times and cycle times.

Bob handed each class member a stopwatch. In less than half an hour, he taught them how to do a formal time and motion study and fill out a special form he provided. In addition to gathering data with stopwatches, Bob explained that inventory levels, travel distances, and floor space data must be collected.

Bob completed his lecture at 4:00 PM. The group enjoyed their day. They were surprised the end of the day had come so quickly. They appreciated the new material they were taught and they appreciated Bob's easy-going style of presentation. Even the skeptical supervisors found the day interesting.

Bob concluded his talks. "I want to thank you for being here today and for your participation. Eight of you will be leaving the group to return to your jobs. The remaining sixteen folks have been assigned to one of the two teams, stamping or assembly. We now have less than four working days to significantly improve those two operations. The stamping team has to cut setup times 80% and the assembly team has to increase pieces per person per day by 50%."

"With all due respect, Bob," one of the shop people spoke up, "We thought today's lessons were very interesting but we don't think your methods will work in our type of factory—we are unique."

"Thanks for your input, but I've heard that talk my whole career. Everyone thinks his or her factory is unique and that Kaizen won't work there. The reality is that manufacturing is a process. I don't care if you're making running shoes, hamster cages, or jet planes—manufacturing is a process of converting raw material to a finished product. Processes are all improved the same way—by discovering where the waste is and permanently eliminating it all. Kaizen is a disciplined approach

143

of waste discovery and permanent removal."

One of the supervisors spoke up. "I really don't see why we have to go through all of this. I've been reading a book about benchmarking. Why doesn't our management benchmark us against our competitors or against similar industries and then just copy what they do?"

Bob smiled, "That's a very good question and that approach could work very well. But let me give you a different perspective. If we can eliminate all the waste here at Sonic, you would be better than any of your competitors. Can you just imagine what this place would look like with ALL waste eliminated?"

It was now almost 4:30 and half the class group was still there talking to Bob. Usually by 4:10 the first shift was out of the plant, but there must have been something magnetic about Bob.

> *It is not enough to be busy.*
> *The question is:*
> *What are we busy about?*
>
> Thoreau

EVENT PHASES

<u>Monday</u>—Kickoff 1-2 days of training begins

<u>Tuesday</u>—Training Completed

<u>Wednesday</u>—Red tag campaign, MUDA hunt, data gathering, begin new process design

<u>Thursday</u>—Implement new process

<u>Friday</u>—Implementation complete, Formal presentation, Celebration

Typical phases during a 5-day Kaizen Event. All events are not 5 days long. Many are completed in 3 or 4 days.

TRAINING CONCEPTS

√ **Kaizen Fundamentals**

√ **Waste (MUDA) Elimination**

√ **Standardization**

√ **Housekeeping (5S)**

√ **Flow Production**

√ **Line Balance**

√ **Time and Motion Study Methods**

Recommended training curriculum to be covered in 8–12 hours prior to start of the actual Kaizen Event.

Discussion—From a LEAN management standpoint: What's going on in this chapter?

In this chapter, Bob Simms has begun to teach the teams about Lean and about Kaizen. In order for these lessons to be effective, he first must convince them they must overcome many *paradigms* that govern their existing processes. The dictionary definition of paradigm is, "One that is worthy of imitation or duplication: beau ideal, example, exemplar, ideal, mirror, model, pattern, standard."

Like the old saying goes, "If you keep doing what you've always done, you'll keep getting what you always got." Many companies have wasteful processes they continue to perform simply because they've always done it that way. It's their paradigm.

When I meet with a new client I like to show them the picture of California as an Island.

Fifteenth Century North American Map Showing California as an Island

There's an interesting story that explains this picture. As you can see, the map depicts California as an island. This map came from fifteenth century cartographers who drew North America for Spanish missionaries. It was a logical assumption based on observation of the Pacific Ocean and the Bay of Baja.

The first missionaries to California took with them huge wooden boats. They hauled those boats across the state and over the mountains, only to find the great California desert—a mighty big beach. The missionaries sent word to the cartographers that the maps were wrong. "California is not an island," they reported, "change the maps."

The cartographers sent back word from Spain. "The map is right. You are in the wrong place."

The amazing thing about this map is that it was used for hundreds of years before explorers finally proved that it was wrong. Bad paradigm.

This is an important abstraction because, just as the Spanish held onto their belief that California was an island *even when confronted with proof*, how many of our beliefs about how our company is run are erroneous—are paradigms?

As part of his training, Bob must give his team "new eyes" to discover for themselves what their paradigms are. That's one of the values of the Red Tag Campaign and Muda hunt. The consultants don't point out the waste in a judgmental fashion; the team discovers it on their own.

CHAPTER 16

DAY TWO—
RED TAGS AND MUDA

Tuesday morning at 7:30 the two teams of eight people each assembled in the conference room. Coffee and doughnuts were arranged in the back of the room.

"Good morning ladies and gentlemen," Bob began. "The first thing we're going to do is divide up into our two groups, stamping and assembly. Larry Smith is going to hand each one of you a pack of red paper tags. I want each of you to go out to your team targets. The stamping team goes out to the stamping department and the assembly team goes out to the assembly department. Once there, I'll give you no more than twenty minutes to put a red tag on anything that will not be used in the coming thirty days. Use the string attached to the tag to apply the tag to equipment, inventory, or trash items. At the end of the twenty minutes, we will ask the people in those areas to look at the items we tagged to make sure we weren't identifying something that will, in fact, be used. After that, we're going to pull all that stuff out. For the moment, we will relocate it all in a central area for either disposal or long-term storage. The important thing is to get it out of the way."

A chorus of complaints exploded. "We need

everything that's out there." "We just had a clean-up campaign last month, there's nothing left to remove." "We tried to do 5S last year and got rid of the trash back then."

"Give me a break," began Bob. "I took a tour early this morning and I saw lots of stuff you don't need. I found an old bicycle missing a back wheel in the stamping department. There was also a floor fan in the corner. We won't need that fan until next summer. Out in the assembly area I saw two supervisor desks but I know there's only one supervisor. Be open-minded. Just take these tags out there and invest twenty minutes of your time. I'm sure you will be surprised how much is out there that you don't need and how much space we will make available when we move the stuff out."

The teams descended on the factory and after a few minutes were laughing out loud at the material they had discovered. The stamping department had dozens of obsolete dies, two ancient stamping presses that hadn't been used in over ten years and rows of old employee lockers filled with junk.

The assembly team discovered the extra supervisor's desk, more chairs than there were employees to sit at, and dozens of huge boxes of work-in-process inventory from products that hadn't been manufactured for years.

Bob had them gather all the red-tagged items in a corner of the warehouse for disposal later. They were all amazed how much they had accumulated in just twenty minutes. The stuff would fill a tractor-trailer. "I'm going to do the red tag approach on my sewing room," one of the ladies on the team remarked. "I wouldn't mind doing this in my back shed," one of the guys offered.

Back in the conference room, Bob got the team ready for the MUDA hunt.

"We're about to search for hidden waste. Remember the Japanese word for waste?" "MUDA," shouted back a team member. "Right you are," said Bob. "The MUDA hunt we're about to do is the most important thing we will do this week." Bob found the list of seven forms of MUDA he had written on the flip chart and taped that page onto the side wall.

- ♦ Muda of overproduction

- ♦ Muda of conveyance

- ♦ Muda of excess inventory

- ♦ Muda of wasted motion

- ♦ Muda of excess processing

- ♦ Muda of waiting

- ♦ Muda of producing failures

Bob explained the definition of each form of waste. He then told the two teams that they had twenty minutes to go back out to their respective areas, stamping and assembly, and hunt for the MUDA there. He had a preprinted form defining each form of MUDA with a space below for writing in what the team discovered.

Bob was confident the teams would have no trouble finding lots of MUDA. His greatest focus was on *overproduction* at Sonic. He had observed that MUDA of overproduction was rampant in both the stamping as well as the assembly area. The stamping department was producing far in excess of the needs of the assembly department because of the large lots dictated by the lengthy setup times. The assembly department was building mountains of work-in-process inventory between each of the operators who were independently working at their own pace, pushing their inventory on to the next operator.

Bob filled out the forms himself, listing only the most critical MUDA observations. He was confident that the teams would find at least six examples of each type of MUDA but he wanted to capture the most significant ones on his own.

> *Our greatest glory is not in never falling down, but in rising every time we fall.*
>
> Confucius

Department *Stamping*	Observer *Bob Simms*
MUDA HUNT	
7 Types of Waste	**List as many examples of each type of MUDA you observe**
1. Overproduction Producing more than is needed before it is needed	*Stamping more parts than assembly needs*
2. Waiting Any nonworking time waiting for tools, supplied parts, etc.	*Operators have to wait till setup man is done before operator can produce*
3. Conveyance Wasted effort to transport materials, parts or finished goods into or out of storage or between processes	*Setup tools nowhere near machines. Raw steel stock far from machines.*
4. Processing Providing higher quality than is necessary, extra operations, etc.	*Stampings need to be deburred. Setups often have to be adjusted.*
5. Inventory Maintaining excess inventory of raw materials, parts in process, or finished goods	*Stamping inventory in excess of assembly dept. needs*
6. Motion Any wasted motion to pick up parts or stack parts. Also wasted walking	*Operators walk to get blanked parts. Parts bins located on floor, requires operators to bend constantly*
7. Correction Repair or rework	*High percentage of defective parts. Total lots rejected.*

MUDA Hunt Form for Stamping Department

Department *Assembly*	Observer *Bob Simms*

MUDA HUNT

7 Types of Waste	List as many examples of each type of MUDA you observe
1. Overproduction Producing more than is needed before it is needed	*W.I.P between operators. Excess finished stock.*
2. Waiting Any nonworking time waiting for tools, supplied parts, etc.	*Operators have to wait for prior operator. Many parts arrive late.*
3. Conveyance Wasted effort to transport materials, parts or finished goods into or out of storage or between processes	*Operators have to get their own parts.*
4. Processing Providing higher quality than is necessary, extra operations, etc.	*Finished assemblies require touch up*
5. Inventory Maintaining excess inventory of raw materials, parts in process, or finished goods	*Stamping inventory in excess of requirements. W.I.P between operator.*
6. Motion Any wasted motion to pick up parts or stack parts. Also wasted walking	*Operators walk to get parts. Parts bins located behind operators requires them to constantly turn. Also "washing machine" motion is required by conveyor layout.*
7. Correction Repair or rework	*High percentage of defective assemblies.*

MUDA Hunt Form for Assembly Department

Bob had both teams put their MUDA observation on flip chart pages that he taped to the conference room walls. "You have completed the most critical exercise of the week. Identifying the sources of waste is 75% of the project. All we need to do is to design new processes that eliminate this waste. I'm confident we can do it and I'll help you.

"At this point in our project, I'm going to separate the two groups to work within the stamping and assembly areas. The stamping team will start the project of reducing setup time and the assembly team will redesign the assembly line. Both teams will also be inventing a "pull" type material delivery system."

> *Do the job,*
> *The work will teach you.*
>
> Bosinsa

Discussion—From a LEAN management standpoint: What's going on in this chapter?

Bob has decided to conduct two Kaizen events simultaneously—one in stamping and one in assembly. This is a bold move, but since Bob is highly experienced, there is a huge potential payback.

The first thing he has the team do is a Red Tag Campaign. This is an excellent way to start because in a very short period of time (twenty minutes) the team accomplished something important. They realize that a lot of the stuff they have been walking past and ignoring for years is of no use for the next month or longer. This is their first experience of taking waste out of their system. They will learn that removing piles of inventory and old stuff just stagnating will improve material flow and quality. After completing the red tag exercise together, they now know that they can function effectively as a team and can make a difference.

One of the operators mentioned that the company had attempted a 5S program but it fell apart after a few months. That is a typical story. 5S cannot succeed when it is presented as a "program." 5S is a key discipline of Kaizen and is typically the *result* of a continuous improvement effort.

Even though the MUDA hunt takes only twenty minutes to complete, it is by far the most important element of the Kaizen event. The whole idea behind the event is that work will become safer, faster, and easier by discovering the waste and permanently eliminating it. The MUDA hunt identifies all the waste. The MUDA hunt is the first step to becoming Lean. This is the company's first recognition that only a fraction of the steps in their processes add value the customer is paying for—the rest is MUDA.

The MUDA hunt forms on pages 153 and 154 are the forms that Bob filled out himself. Fortunately the teams discovered the same MUDA that Bob did when they filled out their forms.

The significant findings in the stamping department were:

♦ The long setup times were causing two types of MUDA: overproduction—since they were trying to amortize long setups with long production runs; And, these long setups created MUDA of the operators waiting for the setup man to make their machines available for production.

♦ The layout required the operators to have MUDA of motion as they had to leave their machines to get parts. The layout required the setup operator to walk to a central location for tools—MUDA of conveyance.

♦ Poor setups were causing two types of MUDA. The punches were not doing a clean job and required deburring that is classified as MUDA of processing. Poor setups were also resulting in rework that is MUDA of correction.

The significant findings discovered in the assembly department were:

- ♦ The imbalance of the assembly line was causing work-in-process to build between operators. This is MUDA of overproduction.

- ♦ This imbalance was also causing operators to wait for each other at times. This is MUDA of waiting.

- ♦ The operators were required to walk to get their own parts. This is MUDA of conveyance.

It is said that Red Tag Campaigns and MUDA hunts give the team members "new eyes" as they have become what is called "factory blind." They could not see all the waste around them.

Every member of the Kaizen team was given red tags to be placed on any objects that will not be used in the next thirty days.

RED TAG CAMPAIGN

A Red Tag is placed on all items that do not belong in this work area

Tagged items are removed from the work space

All Red-Tagged items were brought to a central location for consolidation and disposition

BEFORE

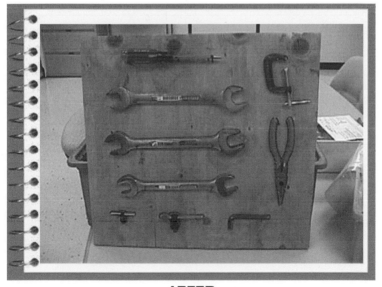

AFTER

**Tool Boards (Shadow Board) Eliminate
Searching or Hunting (Motion Waste) for Tools**

CHAPTER 17

THE ASSEMBLY AREA

Bob met separately with the eight members of the assembly team. In the meantime, the members of the stamping department team were sorting through the red-tagged material and either finding places for it or, more likely, throwing it away.

Bob had the team meet in the assembly area that consisted of five assembly lines manned with an average of ten operators each.

"One of the reasons we chose the assembly area as one of our targets of improvement is because it's the manufacturing department that is closest to our customers. The next step after assembly is shipping. Initially we said that one of the criteria for selecting a process to do Kaizen in is that *the customer must benefit from the improvement.*

Our MUDA hunt showed the following sources of waste in the department:

♦ WIP or work-in-process is built up between each operator (MUDA of overproduction). This WIP is caused by two factors. First is the lot sizing policy. Each operator is building six pieces before passing them to the next operator. We learned during our paper airplane simulation that output goes up a lot when we go from batch processing to one-piece-flow. The second cause of the WIP is the fact that the line isn't balanced. Each operator is supposed to do the same amount of work but it's clear that some of the operations take much more time than others. This is causing several bottlenecks along the line.

♦ Each operator is required to get his or her own materials (MUDA of conveyance)

♦ Each operator keeps tools in a tool box and wastes time searching for the right tool (MUDA of motion)

♦ Each operator is doing *washing machine motions*. That is, since some of their raw materials are located to their side and behind them, operators are constantly twisting their torsos to pick up and then place their parts (MUDA of motion)

♦ The forklift truck is bringing raw material to the head of the assembly line and then traveling all the way to the end of the line to pick up finished goods. If the head and foot were together, as in a U-shaped line, that extra travel would be eliminated. (MUDA of conveyance)

♦ About ten percent of the finished products require rework. The practice has been to make the operator who caused the defect do the repair. In addition to the MUDA of producing defects, is the waste created by stopping the rhythm of the line to do unanticipated repairs.

The first step is to calculate TAKT Time. This is the rhythm of the shop and nothing more than the available time divided by the sales per day.

$$\text{TAKT Time} = \frac{\text{Available Minutes per Day}}{\text{Rate of Sales per Day}}$$

How many minutes of each shift is actual working time?"

One of the supervisors spoke up, "We're here for eight hours, that's 480 minutes but we get 30 minutes for lunch and two 15-minute breaks. So the net working time is 480 minus 30 for lunch and minus another 30 for breaks leaving a net of 420 minutes."

"Good," said Bob. "Now let me ask you what the typical lot size is in assembly. I'm assuming that the lot size is roughly equal to the amount each product sells on a per day basis. What would that lot size typically be?"

"Our lot size is 800 pieces but we work two shifts, so that's 400 pieces per shift" said the same supervisor.

Bob had moved a flip chart into the assembly area and began writing:

$$\text{TAKT Time} = \frac{\underline{\text{Available Minutes per Day}}}{\text{Rate of Sales per Day}}$$

$$= \frac{\underline{\text{420 Minutes per day}}}{\text{400 pieces per day}}$$

$$= 1.05 \frac{\underline{\text{Minutes}}}{\text{Piece}}$$

"We have a big problem right off the bat," began Bob who was writing at the flipchart. All eyes were on him and perplexed about the big problem they couldn't see.

Bob explained, "I've been looking at some of your past production records and they show that your assembly line typically produces one part every 96 seconds. But your Takt Time equals 63 seconds. Your customer is expecting a part every 1.05 minutes which is 63 seconds and you're delivering one every 96 seconds."

"So that's the reason for the ten-hour shifts and Saturdays we've been working the past six weeks," said one of the shop ladies. "At first I enjoyed the money, but those hours are getting to be very difficult."

Bob gave each of the team members a stopwatch and time observation sheets.

"There are eight of you and you have to time each of the ten operators on this progressive assembly line. Split the time studies among the eight of you. I would advise you to take six measurements of each job and come up with an average for each of the ten stations. Then we will diagram your results."

Within a half hour, the time studies were complete and Bob was able to produce a diagram on the flip chart in the assembly area.

Operator	Seconds
1	25
2	17
3	40
4	21
5	93
6	83
7	35
8	55
9	31
10	41
Total	**441**

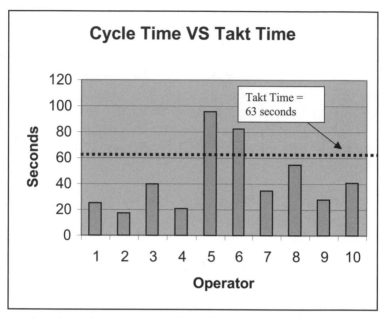

Cycle Time vs. Takt Time before Kaizen

When Bob finished drawing he was able to announce. "We have a terrific opportunity here. We observed ten operators, but they are only doing the work of seven. Here, let me show you."

Bob began calculating on the flip chart.

Crew size = $\dfrac{\text{Total Cycle Time}}{\text{Takt Time}}$ = $\dfrac{441}{63}$ = 7 Operators

Bob explained, "This calculation shows that seven operators are required.

"The bar chart shows us a lot of information. The first thing we can see is that although eight of the ten operators are producing under the 63 second Takt Time, we nevertheless will only get one part every 93 seconds—93 seconds at the operator #5 position is the bottleneck or the choke point on the assembly line.

"The second thing this chart shows us is the source of the entire WIP inventory. Eight of the ten operators are working under the 63 second Takt Time. Rather than sit there idly waiting for other operators to "catch up" they are building and stockpiling inventory between operations.

"By some very simple and quick station rearrangement, we can reduce the line from ten to seven operators as well as eliminate all the inventory."

Bob's chart shows the cycle times of operators #1, #2 and #4 all combine to 63 seconds. That means that the jobs of three operators can be combined into one. That eliminates two operators. Operations #3 and #9 add up to 68 seconds. They can be combined to one operation taking 68 seconds. While 68 seconds is above the 63 second Takt Time, they will be able to find 5 seconds of MUDA to remove later. They still have bottlenecks at operators #5 and #6. All that needs to be done there is move thirty seconds of work from #5 to #7 and then move twenty seconds of work from #6 to #10.

"Some of the operators have more than the 63 seconds of work to do," Bob explained. "If we added up and eliminated all the time being wasted by the operators gathering their own raw materials, searching through their toolboxes for tools, and twisting and reaching for parts, every operator's cycle time will drop significantly."

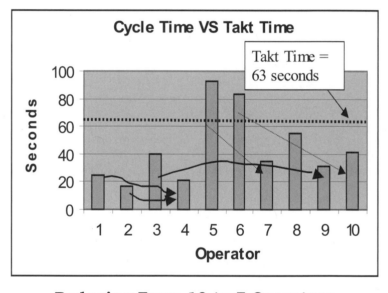

Reducing From 10 to 7 Operators

Operator	Seconds
1	63
2	63
3	63
4	63
5	55
6	63
7	61

Redistribution of Tasks

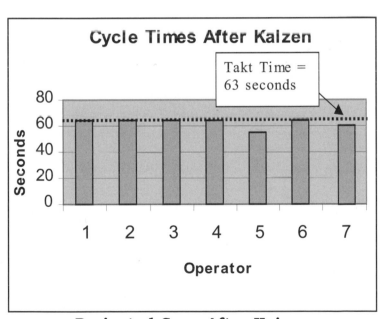

Projected Crew After Kaizen

171

"We have to not only rearrange the operations Bob continued, but also eliminate all the MUDA. That means hanging tools where the operators can conveniently reach them, and having material handlers bring them the raw materials they need by placing them within easy reach.

"One of the other reasons for all the imbalances on the line is the amount of rework many of the operators are performing. One of the cardinal rules of assembly line design is that rework is always separated from assembly work. Initially that could be achieved simply by assigning a special rework operator. Initially we could achieve that quickly by assigning one of the three operators we are eliminating from the line to do rework off the assembly line. But we would need to understand where the rework was coming from and put a permanent end to all the unnecessary rework. One philosophy is called *successive verification*. That's where each operator is responsible to check the work of each prior operator before beginning his or her own tasks. That would mean we would have seven inspectors on the line, as each operator does a bit of inspection as part of the duties.

"I would like you to consider reconfiguring your straight line into a 'U' shape. Your company has kept the manning on your assembly lines constant at ten people per line. This constant manning level limits your flexibility. One of the advantages to a U-shaped cell is the ability to vary the number of workers within the cell to match customer demand. "On a 'U' shaped line you could easily reduce the number of operators. Workers perform an increased number of tasks as demand decreases. The increase in tasks performed is usually accomplished by walking from one section of the cell to another. This would be very difficult on a straight line."

Bob began writing on the flip chart and explained, "I'm about to join the stamping team. In the meantime I'll give you three hours to write a plan to redesign the assembly area. Here are the components of the redesigned area:

♦ Reduce from ten to seven operators
♦ Add a fulltime material handler
♦ Hang all tools in convenient locations
♦ Arrange all raw materials within an easy eighteen-inch reach from all operators
♦ Introduce successive verification
♦ Have all rework performed by just one off-line operator
♦ Decide if a (U) shaped line would be practical.

> *If you want one year of prosperity,*
> *grow grain.*
> *If you want ten years of prosperity,*
> *grow trees.*
> *But if you want one hundred years of prosperity,*
> *Grow People.*
>
> Chinese Proverb

Discussion—From a LEAN management standpoint: What's going on in this chapter?

Bob has discovered that the members of the assembly department, as well as their management, have been living in a world of paradigms. They are surrounded with MUDA but their world looks normal to them.

They have been living with:

♦ Operators fetching their own materials. That would make it a pleasant place to be a material handler, but not very efficient for the assemblers. The material handlers simply drop off a pallet of raw materials somewhere near the assembly line and leave. The operators are then tasked with walking to the material, unbanding, unpacking, and separating. All MUDA.

♦ The operators have been sitting at right angles to the conveyor. In addition to the backbreaking motion is the wasted time in twisting the torso.

♦The most serious problem is the performance against Takt Time. The requirement is one part every 63 seconds and they are completing one part every 96 seconds. In addition to this being the reason for their inability to deliver on time, the imbalance of the line is a major source of work-in-process inventory.

♦ Not only is the line imbalanced, they have ten operators doing the work of seven.

In order for the team to "Speak with Data," the operators are taught to calculate Takt Time and the use of stopwatch time studies for use in balancing the assembly line.

Kaizen Teams Learned to do Time Studies

Assembly line operator must twist her body (a "washing machine motion") in order to place parts onto conveyor.

Haphazard location of tools caused MUDA of motion. Tooling shadow boards and location labeling eliminated that wasted motion.

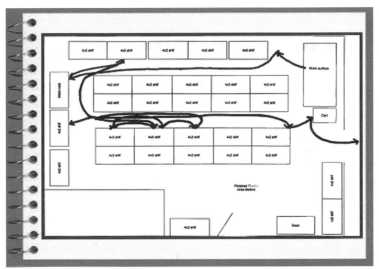

Spaghetti Diagram in an assembly area revealed the shortcoming of the layout. This exhibit shows that, before Kaizen, the product traveled a total of 571 feet.

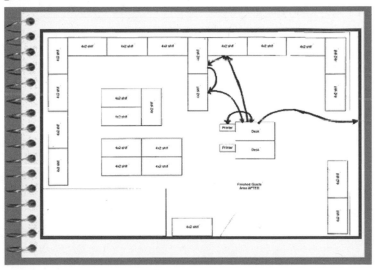

After Kaizen, travel distance was reduced from 571 to 46 feet, a 90% improvement.

177

CHAPTER 18

THE STAMPING
DEPARTMENT

Bob left the assembly team and, by the time he arrived at the stamping department, they had made disposition of all the red-tagged materials and had begun a general tidying up of the area.

"You guys have done a great job, the place is looking better already. Our main task now is to reduce the setup time from 90 minutes to under 30 minutes. To begin, I want to explain the difference between *internal* and *external* activities. Simply stated, internal activities are those that can be performed only while the machine is *not* running. External activities can be performed while the machine is running. For example, you can't exchange dies while the machine is running. So die exchange would be classified as an internal operation. On the other hand, activities such as getting die sets from the tool room, gathering paperwork, gathering tools, and filling out paperwork are all external operations.

"The discipline we are about to practice is called *Single Minute Exchange of Dies*, or SMED for short. It was developed by the Toyota Corporation. Using SMED they were able to reduce their setup times from over twelve hours to less than ten minutes.

"I think that when you study the die exchange here at Sonic, you will see that many activities that should be done externally are, in fact, done internally. I want two of the eight of you to use your time observations forms and do a complete study of a typical die exchange. Since these exchanges typically take 90 minutes, you should be able to complete the time study as well as the Internal vs. External analysis within two hours of the start of the next die exchange. I need one of you to draw what we call a *spaghetti* diagram. It's also sometimes called a *Dance Chart*. All it is is a sketch of the steps the setup man takes as he walks during his setup. You will show a line going from the press to the tool room and then a line from the tool room back to the press and so forth. When the sketch is done, you will have many lines going back and forth. It will look like spaghetti.

"The remaining five of you will be observing the setup man and making up a list of what I call *'Why Questions'*. What that means is that while you observe his activities, you are to write a list of questions that begin with the word *Why*.

"Some question could be something like, 'Why did the setup man not get the tools he needed before the setup began, while the press was in operation? Or, 'Why didn't the setup man have to go to the die set room while the press was still running to get the next die he was going to use?' "

"I'm going to return to the assembly team and I'll be back here in three hours. At that time I would like to see your spaghetti diagram, your internal vs. external summary and your list of Why questions."

> *People don't resist change.*
> *They resist being changed.*
>
> Anon

CHAPTER 19

ASSEMBLY IMPROVEMENTS

The assembly team redid the cycle time versus Takt Time chart showing only seven operators and all operations within the 63-second takt time. They assumed one of the three eliminated operators would do all the material handling and another would do all the rework.

They showed Bob a simple sketch of a tool holder consisting of nothing more than a one foot square of plywood with some nails to hold the tools convenient to the operator. They made a sketch showing the seven operators arranged into a "U" shaped assembly line that took up less than one-half the space of the original line. The original line was arranged in a straight line and had spaces of about four feet between operators. This not only took up too much room, it allowed for the accumulation of work-in-process inventory. They actually needed much of the four feet between operators since they were producing with lots of six. By converting to one-piece flow, the operators could be relocated so that they were almost elbow-to-elbow.

"I like the work you've done so far," Bob said. "And now we have to turn your dreams into reality. For the rest of the afternoon I would like this team to discuss your observations and proposals with the ten operators. We will need their input and their patience with the new configuration as we debug it for the next few days. In addition to discussions with the assembly people, you will need to begin making your tool boards and gathering materials to build your (U) shaped line. Remember Kaizen is a low-cost, no-cost approach to improvement. I'm sure we could get catalogs of some very fancy workstations and spend lots of money. Unfortunately we have until Friday to get your new line and your new workstations into operations. We have to scrounge for materials that will get us up and running in the next three days".

One of the operators stood to ask Bob a question. "I admit I was very skeptical about all this on Monday. I'm now convinced that we will make major improvements but for the life of me I don't understand why we have to get this done by Friday. We're doing everything in rush mode. It would be so much better if we could do this project over a few weeks."

"There's a simple explanation," began Bob. "By creating the ambitious goals to be achieved in only five days, we created a crisis. People create great things during a crisis. Studies have shown that the mind is sharpened and cooperation increases in a crisis. As for stretching the project out over several weeks, you've had several years to improves things here at Sonic and I don't think you've improved many things."

*The quality of a person's life
is in direct proportion to their
commitment to excellence, regardless
of their chosen field of endeavor.*

V. Lombardi

CHAPTER 20

STAMPING IMPROVEMENTS

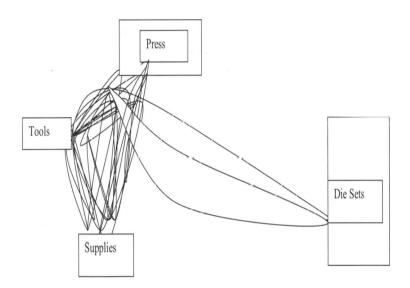

When Bob arrived back at the stamping department, he found the team studying the spaghetti diagram. "Does that diagram give you any great ideas?" he asked.

"Lots of great ideas," came back the reply. John Johnson the stamping supervisor rose and faced Bob. "I've worked in this department for seven years and until I looked at this diagram I hadn't realized how much wasted motion this layout is causing us.

"Right off the bat I can see that if I put the tool cabinet on wheels, I could cut out about a third of the wasted walking. Each of our press families are dedicated to specific dies but we keep all dies centralized in one room. The same goes for the associated supplies. With very little effort we could locate the die sets and supplies adjacent to the presses they serve. That will cut down a tremendous amount of unnecessary walking."

Bob was beaming. "I see you got maximum benefit from the spaghetti diagram. What did you learn from the Internal vs. External study and from the *Why* questions?"

One of the women on the team handed him a copy of the time summaries.

	Current Observed Time	Projected Time
Internal Time	90 Min.	16 Min.
External Time	0 Min.	12 Min.
TOTAL	90 Min.	28 Min.

"We were surprised to see that we might be able to beat the 30-minute target. These improved numbers assume that the room gets rearranged

and we convert some internal activities to external.

"We also got some good ideas from our 'Why List."

She handed Bob the list:

♦ Why can't all paperwork be located at the
  press before die exchange begins?

♦ Why can't the new die be located at the
  press before the exchange begins?

♦ Why can't the old die be returned to the die
  room after new die is in operation?

♦ Why are all dies centrally located'?

♦ Why can't dies be stored near the machines
  they serve?

♦ Why can't tools be permanently hung from
  the presses?

♦ Why are there so many sizes of fasteners
  used throughout the operation resulting in
  many different sized wrenches? Can they be
  standardized so that there are only two or
  three used?

♦ Why can't pneumatic tools be used to replace wrenches?

♦ The press operator is idle during the die
  exchange. Why can't he assist the setup
  man during the die exchange?

Bob studied the list. "This is a terrific list. Good work. In the current operation there are no external operations and the total die exchange takes 90 minutes. By rearranging your room, you have projected a very large timesavings. In your projection, you show that the setup man takes only twenty-eight minutes to complete a die exchange but the important thing is that you have reduced internal time to only sixteen minutes. In the old method, the press was actually shut down for ninety minutes and you now project that it will only be shut down for sixteen minutes. That's a reduction from ninety to sixteen minutes. That is an 82% improvement. Congratulations.

"It's getting to be the end of our second day. I suggest we focus tomorrow on all your room rearrangements and then we can begin perfecting the new system to see how close to the 16-minute projection we can get. You know those pit crews that change tires and do refueling on formula and Indy cars in less than ten seconds took a long time to perfect their act and they do it with lots of practice and lots of new refinements."

Bob and Larry were driving in together during this week. This gave them time during the drive to work in the morning to plan the upcoming day and review the day's progress on the way home.

They rode in Bob's car. It was Tuesday evening on the drive home and Bob was reflecting. "Well Larry, we're through two days and I think we're making great progress. You have a great team at Sonic, Larry."

"I know they're a great team but it took you and your Kaizen tools to draw them out. I can't believe how many great ideas they've come up with."

"Listen, Larry, the hard part is behind us. We've completed our analysis and have developed an attack plan both for assembly as well as stamping. This is Tuesday night and we have until Friday to complete the project. That means that we have just two days—Wednesday and Thursday—to implement our plans. While the plans are perfectly sound, I can guarantee that they won't work perfectly. Remember I told you that one of the underlying principles of Kaizen is to create a nonjudgmental environment? Well here's where we get to prove that. We have to expect that things are about to go wrong. I really don't care if we make mistakes as long as we learn from those mistakes and as long as we keep moving forward. As long as we keep moving forward, we can make progress by just making corrections as we move ahead."

"I wish Mr. Brady shared those philosophies," commented Larry. "That guy criticized everything. It got to the point where nobody made suggestions or took initiatives to introduce even the simplest change. Brady would pounce on every error and misstep. He destroyed all initiative."

Bob was smiling while listening to Larry's description of Brady. Bob began, "Brady's learning a lot this week. Maybe this week will teach him lessons about how to treat people and how to engage their hearts as well as their minds.

"Tomorrow, Wednesday, is a big day. We have to re-arrange both the assembly department as well as stamping. My goal is to have that completed by the day's end. Then we can spend all day Thursday smoothing things out. In addition to helping me with the two teams, I would like you to get started on preparing a PowerPoint presentation for Friday. We will need before and after photographs of the stamping and assembly areas. Since the rooms will be arranged tomorrow you should get in there early in the morning with your digital camera and get pictures before things start changing.

"This PowerPoint will serve many functions. First, it will preserve a record of this week. Future Kaizen teams will be using that as a guide. Second, it could be shown to the rest of the factory so that they understand what our program is all about. And the third function is most important— to give recognition to our Kaizen teams. On Friday they will present their achievements to Brady and I promise you he will be appropriately grateful for all the progress they made".

> *Unless you try to do something*
> *beyond what you have already mastered*
> *You will never grow.*
>
> R.W. Emerson

Discussion—From a LEAN management standpoint: What's going on in this chapter?

Bob is deploying the SMED disciplines to improve the operation of the stamping department. The three key tools are:

♦ The spaghetti diagram. Some people also call it a "Dance Chart." It's called that because it looks like the diagrams used by ballroom dance instructors to show students where to place their feet for different types of dance.

♦ The "internal vs. external" study. This is a commonsense method of assuring that much preparation for the changeover occurs while the machine is still operating.

♦ The "Why List." It is especially useful to bring people onto the SMED team that have no familiarity with that department. They will notice things that the normal residents have taken for granted.

There are two everyday examples of the SMED discipline applied. The first and most obvious is in formula car races. It's not necessarily the fastest car that wins the race. The car that spends the least amount of time at the pit stop has a tremendous advantage.

If you had to change all four tires on your car, refuel, drink seven ounces of water, and clean your windshield, it would take hours. But all those activities are done in under ten seconds. Naturally they can achieve that because not just one person is involved—it's a team. Aside from that, the other reasons for the quickness are that everything is prepared in advance and that the team practices. They practice a lot. Their practice results in *continuous improvement.*

The other everyday example of SMED disciplines is in the theater. When the curtain comes down on act one and goes up to begin act two revealing an entirely new set and different costumes for the actors, it's obvious that they didn't construct new sets and recostume in three minutes. The new set was prepared to drop into place, stagehands were ready to do the replacements, and the actors wore the new costumes under the old ones.

The concepts of having tools prestaged and having an experienced well-practiced team at the ready can be applied in most factories.

At this point in the Kaizen event, the team should be ready to begin preparation of the PowerPoint presentation. As stated in the chapter, the presentation is useful to capture and memorialize the elements of the event. These PowerPoints serve as excellent sources of training materials for future teams as well as outstanding promotional materials for investors and customers.

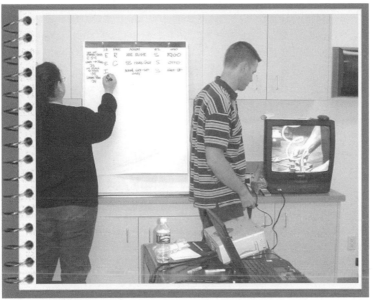

SMED study using video. Once the setup process is captured on video, it can be carefully analyzed in the office.

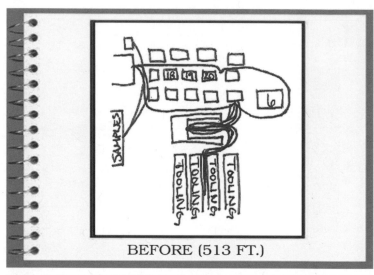

BEFORE (513 FT.)

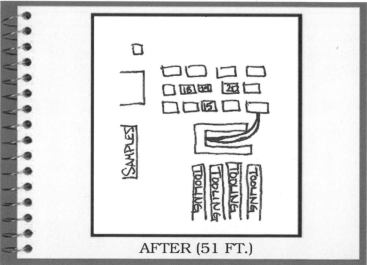

AFTER (51 FT.)

This Spaghetti Diagram shows that locating setup tools in several locations created excessive walking. In the improved layout some tools were brought to a central location and others were permanently located at the machines where they were used. This relocation of tools reduced travel distance by 91%.

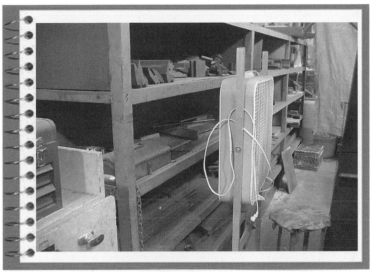

BEFORE

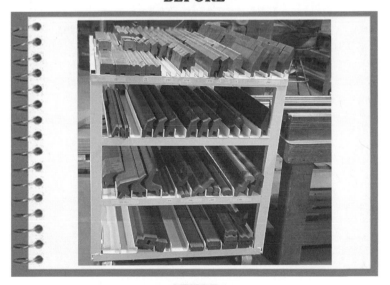

AFTER

Many of the tools that had been stored in a centralized location were relocated to positions adjacent to each machine where they were used.

197

The **MUDA** hunt revealed that the bolts that fastened the die sets in the presses were tightened with a ratchet wrench. Switching to a pneumatic wrench was simple since each machine had an air supply. Fastening time was reduced 90%.

CHAPTER 21

MAINTENANCE

On Wednesday morning while Larry was taking photographs and the teams were getting ready to start moving things around, Bob had a meeting with Benny DeVito, the first-shift supervisor, Jim Cory, the shearing supervisor, and Paul Johnson, his maintenance man.

"Do you guys have any kind of a preventive maintenance program in this stamping room?" Bob asked.

Benny DeVito answered, "We use what we call *breakdown maintenance* here at Sonic. What that means is when something breaks down we fix it. We don't have time to do preventive maintenance—our machines are all fully utilized. Jim Brady's chart shows that our machine utilization averages 85%."

Bob smiled at Benny's answer and asked, "I saw all of Jim's charts and they make very little sense to me. Let me ask you something. If you subtracted the time the machines spend being repaired and subtract the time the machines make defects, and then subtract the time the machines are being setup at 15 minutes a shot, what percentage do you think the machines are actually running?"

"I never thought of it that way," Benny just stood there scratching his head under his John Deere gimme hat. He continued, "If you put it that way, I doubt if we use our machines 25% of the time to make parts."

"That's pretty much what I figured," replied Bob. "You guys want to do a worthwhile exercise and collect that information. It's not hard; just hang some check sheets on clipboards next to each machine and after a week you will have some very valuable data that could point you toward some real problem solving.

"We can't create a preventive maintenance program by Friday but there are some positive actions we can take right away.

"Have any of you guys ever heard of TPM? It stands for *Total Productive Maintenance*. It's a Japanese discipline designed to assure that machines are always available for use. Most of the discipline deals with preventive maintenance. I want to explain one component of TPM called *Autonomous Maintenance*. It's a great method for involving the machine operators in maintenance.

"It works pretty much like the way a car owner takes care of his end of automobile maintenance. The average driver periodically changes his oil, checks tire inflation, and replaces the tires when they need it. In addition, he maintains his various fuel levels. But when he hears that funny noise in the engine or when he notices the car pulling sharply to the right when braking, he goes to his mechanic and describes the problem.

"I suggest we do something like this with the shearing machines." Bob turned toward Jim Cory, the shearing supervisor. "Jim, how many maintenance responsibilities do your operators have?" Jim quickly replied," The only thing close to maintenance that they do is sweep the floor."

"Sweeping the floor is a good start," began Bob. "I suggest you explain the automobile analogy to the operators and give them a logbook to begin recording their observations for the maintenance department. In addition to a logbook, you might even consider giving them yellow tags. You can tell them if they notice something wrong with their machine, they could put a yellow tag on that item. Tell them that once they place the tag on the machine, only they have the authority to remove the tag. And that tag can't be removed until the operator is satisfied that the issue was corrected.

"These tags could be on safety items like frayed wires or leaking oil. Or they could be on legitimate maintenance items like broken gages or cracked housings. The more you involve the operators, the better your program will be. Once you get this autonomous maintenance program under way, you can begin a proper preventive maintenance program. You'll be amazed that, by planning and scheduling your maintenance downtime instead of reacting to unanticipated corrective maintenance, your machine availability will soar to new heights".

Discussion—From a LEAN management standpoint: What's going on in this chapter?

Bob has discovered that the factory is in a state of disrepair. Although all the machines run much of the time, all the yellow tags dramatically show that there are breakdowns and safety problems just waiting to happen. The situation is pretty serious, the supervisor has estimated that the machines only run 25% of the time when breakdowns, slowdowns, and setups are all considered.

Bob knows that it would be impossible to install a proper maintenance program within a week. The yellow tag campaign is vital:

♦ It illuminates all the problems. These tags should remain in place until the person who put them there is satisfied that the problem has been resolved. It also makes it pretty hard for the boss to ignore the problem.

♦ It allows the magnitude of the situation to be quantified. All the yellow tag items can now be summarized in one report and the labor, as well as material, can be estimated.

At this point it would be wise to call the equipment manufacturers in to bring the equipment back to specification, train the local personnel on maintenance requirements, and assure that adequate spare parts are available in the facility.

Yellow Tag Campaign on an injection molding press. Tags were placed to highlight such problems as frayed wires, cracked bracket, and a loose handle.

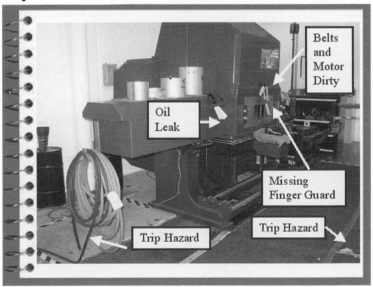

Yellow Tags in the Stamping Department

CHAPTER 22

DROWNING IN INVENTORY

Bob left the stamping department and walked over to Larry Smith's office where Larry was preparing the PowerPoint presentation for Friday.

Larry used the digital camera to take the "before" picture's of the stamping and assembly departments and was inserting them into the presentation.

Bob sat down in the chair next to Larry's desk and began, "Larry, I want to discuss the subject of inventory with you for a few minutes. Why don't you put the PowerPoint aside for now?" Larry pushed his chair back from his desk and swiveled it to face Simms.

"You know, Bob, until lately I *liked* having lots of inventory. I really appreciated all the stock in finished goods because I could guarantee any customer that he could get any product in our catalog within ten days. I liked having lots of inventory after shearing and stamping because I had frequent machine shutdowns and long setup times. The assembly area often ran out of parts to assemble the latest order. Rather than send the assembly department home, I would just have them assemble whatever we had parts for regardless of whether or not we had an order for that product. Our inattention to inventory was never a problem until lately. Now it seems that we're drowning in inventory. The funny thing is that we have lots of inventory of parts we don't need and we're spending a fortune on overtime and expedited air shipments for parts we don't have. I'm coming to the conclusion that I have to switch from my *Just-in-Case* inventory system to a *Just-in-Time* system."

Larry's office had a large window that looked out into the factory. Bob stood up and pointed out the window into the factory. "You have allowed the inventory to grow to a ridiculous level. and I doubt if any of you realize how much this is costing the company. I think your high inventory level is the biggest problem facing you. Let me give you some perspectives.

"Your inventory levels are hurting quality. In your high inventory environment, defects are typically found only a long time after the damage actually occurred. That makes it difficult to find the real cause.

"This makes the situation even worse when you find defects. Those events probably first trigger fire fighting and expediting rather than getting down to the root cause. In a low inventory environment, when the defect is found, you are still producing the product at the first operation. In my opinion, it's not possible to have very high quality unless you have low inventories.

Then Bob asked, "Do you think it is coincidence that the Japanese have both the lowest inventory and the highest quality?

"Your inventory is having a major effect on your margins. You just said that now that you haven't been shipping on time you are resorting to overtime and premium freight. These kinds of unplanned expenses shrink your margins and reduce your ability to reduce your prices.

"You said that you enjoyed the comfort of having every part in stock so that whatever your customer ordered, you had it available. The reality, Larry, is that the greater your inventory, the *longer* will be your leadtime. In a high inventory environment you will find it very, very hard to compete against faster competitors and quote shorter than achievable lead times, or Sonic will continue to maintain finished goods inventories based upon your typically unreliable forecasts.

In a low inventory environment, you can produce to order and meet quoted lead times, and not have to rely upon forecasts. You can have the luxury of producing just what is needed.

"I think we both agree that there are two types of forecasts—*lucky and lousy.*"

Your inventory has an effect on Investments," Bob reminded Larry. In many cases your machines are not capable of dealing with the peak load occurring during the month, although on average you probably have excess capacity. In a high inventory environment like this, critical products arrive only in large batches and then have to be processed quickly. That causes a relatively long peak load, triggering the request for more machine capacity to accommodate the peak load. In the low inventory environment, the load is more uniformly spread due to smaller batches flowing through the plant and additional machinery is not required. I think you were able to see that in our paper airplane simulation. I'm quite sure that your inventory has an impact on *Due-Date Performance.* In general, due-date performance is perceived as being dependent upon our customers changing their requirements, vendors performing poorly, and forecasts that are unreliable. In a high inventory environment, production lead times are longer, requiring a longer horizon forecast, the quality of which deteriorates quickly with its horizon. Furthermore, customers tend to change their minds during the longquoted lead times providing additional problems. Finally, due to the inherent changes, your demands upon your vendors are constantly changing. You already told me how frustrated your suppliers are with you. In a low inventory environment, you can work either with real orders or at least with a more accurate forecast improving your due-date performance.

"Your Inventory affects your *Quoted Lead Times.* In general, it is thought that short lead times require high work in process and finished goods inventories.

Lead times and work-in-process are the same and a company should hold finished goods inventory proportionate to its work-in-process inventory to cover variances in lead time plus demand and supply. If we reduce our WIP inventory levels, we increase our responsiveness since these are determined by the work-in-process levels and you can reduce your finished goods inventory."

Larry sat there, stunned. "Okay, okay I can see that I'm drowning in inventory. I can also see that it would be wonderful to reduce our inventory levels so that the money invested in *stagnating* inventory could be moved into a *cash* account. I know that in strict accounting terms this would translates to a reduction in working capital on the balance sheet and an increase in return on assets. But where do we begin?"

Kind words can be short and easy to speak, but their echoes are truly endless.

Mother Theresa

CHAPTER 23

FLOW

"There's an old saying, Larry, that goes 'You can't push a string.' Obviously, if there was a string lying here on your desk, you could pull it easily across the desk. But it would be difficult to push it. What we have to create at Sonic is a *Pull System,*" Bob said.

"We need to create a synchronous flow of material across your value stream and eliminate your need for buffers. Right now that's hard to imagine, but I think we can come up with something and put it into effect before Friday. Rather than introduce a massive change, I think we should introduce this pull system on just one product family. Which family of products goes through every department and also represents significant volume?"

Larry thought for just a moment and offered, "Our Radiance loudspeakers represent about 60% of our volume. If we could streamline Radiance production, that would be a major achievement."

Bob walked to the chalkboard in Larry's office and began to draw. "Let's design a system for Radiance parts and then implement it. It will take about a month before the system is de-bugged, at which time we can rollout the new production control method across all products. In an ideal world the rate of all production would exactly equal the rate of sales. In that ideal world, every time a customer purchased one part, the factory would produce one part and our suppliers would ship us all the pieces we need to make just one part. That would be done with zero inventories. Now we both know that's impossible, but let's see how close to that vision we can come."

Bob vocalized his plan: "There are five models in the Radiance family of speakers. We could set up a min-max inventory in the finished goods area and when it was time to replenish, we would deliver a signal to get more speakers from the assembly department. This signal could be nothing more than a piece of paper showing that 'Radiance Model #1 is down to 100 pieces and we need 500 pieces to replenish the finished goods stock. This piece of paper is called a Kanban. Kanban is a Japanese word meaning *signal.*

"This system I'm describing would require the assembly department to maintain an inventory of it's own a kind of *supermarket* of Radiance speakers. This supermarket would have the five kinds of Radiance speakers on shelves. It would work like a real supermarket. When the cans of a particular type of soup along the aisle run down to a certain level, an employee is required to go to the warehouse at the back of the store and replenish that row of cans and bring that row up to the original stocking level. That's how the Radiance assembly department supermarket would work. When a replenishment point was hit for one of the models, a signal (Kanban) would trigger an order to assemble more of those speakers.

"This would require the assembly department to go to the stamping department who would have a similar supermarket of stamped parts that they would maintain with their Kanban system. Since there are four stamped parts for each speaker and we need to maintain parts for five models, we need twenty parts bins to maintain.

"We can start building the stamping department's supermarket immediately. All we need are twenty bin locations and two types of Kanban cards. One color card will be used as "withdrawal' Kanbans. Whenever the assembly department withdraws parts from the stamping supermarket they issue a withdrawal card. This card will show, how many parts were taken to assembly. When a particular bin in the assembly department reaches a trigger point, a (production) Kanban card of a different color would be issued to the stamping department to signal them to produce the replenishment quantity."

"Bob, let me stop you right there," Larry interrupted. " I don't think this system has a chance of working here. Our shears constantly break down and we still have to rely on marketing forecasts."

"You're right about the shear reliability," Bob began. "With this system you have no choice but to get a good corrective and preventive maintenance system going.

"In the past you were able to live with all the

breakdowns, but by limiting your WIP you will have no choice but to keep your machines running. As for the marketing forecasts, I don't think that will be much of a problem. What if we invented a magic machine that made a complete loudspeaker at a push of a button in three seconds? Then you wouldn't need marketing forecasts would you? Well this system simulates that condition. You will be reacting to marketing demands by maintaining a small inventory of all critical parts throughout your operation."

Larry scratched his head. "What about our MRP system?" he asked.

"I'm not suggesting you scrap your MRP system," Bob began. "But what I am suggesting is that you ignore those pieces of your MRP system that are now scheduling shearing, stamping, and assembly.

"I'm looking forward to tomorrow, Thursday. We should be mostly through with our implementation of changes by the end of the day. I'm especially interested to see what the new assembly area looks like."

Things turn out best for the people who make the best out of the way things turn out.

Art Linkletter

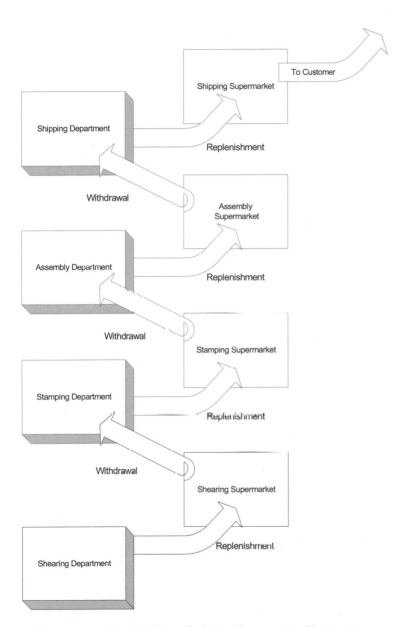

Supermarket Material Delivery Pull System

Discussion—From a LEAN management standpoint: What's going on in this chapter?

In the 1980s, the American car manufacturers received a wake-up call from Japan. Our consumers were getting fed up with American defect-laden, gas-guzzlers and were getting very interested in what Toyota had to offer. GM, Ford, and Chrysler responded with an approach that was doomed to failure from the start.

GM in particular invested a fortune in automation and robotics. At that time, Manufacturing Resources Planning (MRP) was in vogue as a method of controlling production. Both of these tactics failed. The automation turned out to be inflexible and the MRP system encouraged huge increases in inventory.

Kanban Cards Used in a Two Bin System

In the meantime, the Toyotas and Nissans were getting really good at deploying the TPS (Toyota Production System) which focused heavily on increasing the velocity of production, fully engaging the workforce, and ruthlessly assaulting all kinds of waste.

The Toyota Production System did not rely on computer based production control systems like MRP. Their approach was very simple and very effective—it just used cards.

These are photographs of actual Kanban cards. A Kanban card must, at a minimum, contain four pieces of information: part number, description, quantity, and location. The cards in the photos are for a part called the "2001 Aftermarket Box" and the parts are to be located in the warehouse supermarket.

These particular cards are part of a "two bin system." Every part in this supermarket is stored in two identical bins. Each container in this example initially has 400 parts in them. Parts are withdrawn from one container until that container is empty. That signals that a replenishment point has been hit and a new quantity of 400 Aftermarket Boxes has to be obtained. In the meantime, withdrawals will be made from the second bin.

There are a number of ways the Kanban card can be used as a signal. The simplest way is for the card to by physically taken to the department that supplies Aftermarket Boxes. Or the Kanban card can simply be scanned and the sig nal electronically delivered to the producing department.

If the producing department is an outside supplier, the Kanban card can be faxed to them as a signal to deliver 400 units.

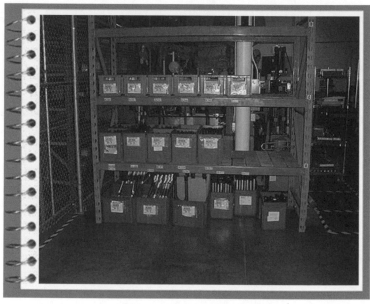

This is a Photo of a Supermarket Using a Two-Bin System.

CHAPTER 24

THE IMPROVED
ASSEMBLY AREA

Thursday morning Bob and Larry entered the assembly area and were very pleased with the site before them. The team had radically changed one of the assembly lines. It was arranged into a "U" shape and had only seven operators. Each operator had a board within easy reach containing the tools needed at that station. There was an outline drawn on the board around each tool so that missing tools could be easily identified.

All materials used at each station were located within an eighteen-inch reach. There was no longer any need for operators to look for tools or to employ the washing machine motions when turning to get parts.

Bob walked over to the line and asked one of the operators, "How do you like this new setup?" The operator looked up from her work and replied, "When we were first told that seven of us would be doing the work of ten, I thought the idea was crazy. But now that we've tried it for a few hours, I think I like it better. Before the line was 'U' shaped, I was isolated from most of the other operators. With these new arrangements, I can see every person on the line and we can now communicate with each other. I like that a lot. The line still isn't balanced—

some of us are doing more work than others and some WIP is building up. We are working together to redistribute the work so that each station takes the same amount of time—63 seconds."

Bob was beaming; not only had they produced a line with 30% fewer operators, it looked like the new line took up half the space of the other lines in the assembly area. He turned to Larry.

"I'm happy to see that the operators are working among themselves to rebalance the assembly line. It certainly doesn't take a degree in industrial engineering to balance an assembly line. Hopefully, they will view line balance as an ongoing activity as the line continues to improve its cycle time."

CHAPTER 25

THE IMPROVED STAMPING DEPARTMENT

Bob and Larry entered the stamping department and found the Kaizen team looking at the "Why List" printed on the flipchart.

- Why can't all paperwork be located at the press before die exchange begins? √

- Why can't the new die be located at the press before the exchange begins? √

- Why can't the old die be returned to the die room after new die is in operation?

- Why are all dies centrally located? √

- Why can't dies be stored near the machines they serve? √

- Why can't tools be permanently hung from the presses?

- Why are there so many sizes of fasteners used throughout the operation resulting in many different sized wrenches? Can they be standardized so that there are only two or three used?

• Why can't pneumatic tools be used to replace wrenches? √

• The press operator is idle during the die exchange. Why can't he assist the setup man during the die exchange?

Bob addressed the team, "So what progress have you made?" John Johnson, the stamping department supervisor, replied, "We are very close to our target setup time of 28 minutes. We used the spaghetti diagram to completely rearrange our storage of tools and supplies so that everything is kept close to the machines. If you notice five of the nine 'Why Questions' have a check mark after them. That means that the condition was corrected. We're still working on the other four which should get us down to our target value."

CHAPTER 26

FOLLOWING UP

Bob and Larry were driving home Thursday evening. Larry was euphoric. "I can't believe what you were able to achieve in only four days. We now know how to reduce setup times, we know how to use thirty percent fewer people and half the space in assembly, we have the beginnings of a pull type material systems, and now have operators involved in maintenance."

Bob was expertly maneuvering his BMW through the turns in the country lanes on the way back to their development. He had a satisfied look on his face as well. "It's too early to celebrate, Larry. A lot can go wrong if you don't carefully follow through on what we kicked off this week.

"One of the things most companies start their LEAN conversion with is what's called a LEAN promotions office. This is a central control point for all LEAN improvement activities. It's not too late to start one here at Sonics and it looks like that function will be a major component of your job in the future. The function is not only responsible for initiating improvements, but for follow through as well. It is the responsibility of the Lean promotion officer as well as the executive team to perform this activity.

"Tomorrow afternoon the team will make a formal presentation to Brady on all that you've achieved. You will also report on things that you did not achieve this week and that need to be completed in the future. These are typically delineated in the format of 'who-what-when.' People must be held accountable for their commitments.

"One of the things we have to develop on Friday is your new metrics. I think Brady has learned that his metrics were of no use to improving anything. Now is the time to think of new, actionable metrics. In the assembly area, you need to measure performance against takt time as well as pieces per person per day. In the stamping area, you need to measure setup times. In the shear area, you need to measure how often machines break down and how long the repair takes. These metrics should not be located in Brady's office; they shouldn't be located in anyone's office. They should be conspicuously posted in the areas they measure. And most important—people must be held accountable for their performance.

"As Lean promotions officer you, as well as company management, have to make follow-up a major part of your jobs. In addition to monitoring people's commitments for future tasks and performance of key metrics, you and your people must monitor housekeeping.

"Housekeeping must be maintained. The simplest method of achieving this maintenance is with posted photographs of what the area looked like immediately after the Kaizen event. This serves as a constant reminder of how things must be maintained.

"In addition to follow up activities, the management must get involved in follow through activities. The initial vision was established with the Value Stream Map. The *Future State* depicts what the future facility will look like. Once the initial momentum is established, additional events can be scheduled and the participants from the first Kaizen team can assist future teams."

They were pulling into the development. Larry turned to Bob and began, "Bob, you don't have to worry about my following up and following through."

"I'm not worried about that Larry, I'm worried about what can go wrong. The Kaizen Event is a terrific way to overcome organizational inertia. However, cultural barriers to change are difficult to eliminate, ESPECIALLY among middle managers. The typical middle manager enjoys the comforts of buffer inventory, nondocumented, uncontrolled processes, and long production runs. On top of that, we have the concept of *entropy*. It almost seems as if factories *want to be screwed up*. The strongest weapon against collapse of the improvement effort is for the executives to routinely and frequently tour the factory.

"In our culture, there is often an aversion to touring the factory and a strong desire to review (after the fact) factory performance in the comfort of the conference room surrounded with reports and graphs. In excellent factories, when production problems occur, the executives go to the factory floor. In poorly run facilities, when production problems occur, the executives go to the conference room to announce, 'It's not my fault!'

"Continuous improvement cannot be delegated. It is a principal role of the senior executive team. The Kaizen events we conducted here this week can either be the exciting beginning of tremendous performance gains or a complete waste of everyone's time if it is not given sufficient follow up."

Bob pulled into Larry's driveway. "Go enjoy your family, tomorrow is a big day. We need to develop those metrics, make the presentation to Brady and hopefully get him to lead a well-deserved celebration."

---

*Treat people as if they were
what they ought to be
and you will help them become
what they are capable of being.*

Goethe

AFTER THE EVENT

Follow Up

√ Hold people accountable for their commitments.

√ Hold people accountable for their performance.

Follow Through

√ Keep eyes on the targets

Use Value Stream Map for focus on the future state

The Kaizen Event is only the first step in the Lean conversion.

Discussion—From a LEAN management standpoint: What's going on in this chapter?

Larry needs to follow up and follow through. That means he needs to put some tools in place for that purpose.

Kicking off a Lean implementation in a factory is something like planting a sapling in your back yard. If you nurture the delicate sapling: water it, fertilize it, keep the weeds away, it will grow into a magnificent tree. But if during those first few months you neglect it, it will probably die. It's like that with Lean. The momentum and excitement gained immediately after a Kaizen event won't last long unless management nurtures the situation.

One of the most useful tools is the Improvement Plan written in a "What-Who-When" format. In addition to showing the action to be taken, the plan should also list the problem or waste that the action will eliminate. This is an important discipline. Many times, an action is taken and people forget what the problem was that the action was supposed to eliminate. In the Improvement Plan below, the first column shows that.

This plan must be conspicuously posted in the area for everyone to see. This becomes a "living document." That is, as new opportunities are discovered, they get added to the list. Items are continuously taken off the list as the actions get completed, and new items continuously appear. The improvement plan is a key continuous improvement tool.

IMPROVEMENT PLAN			
Waste	**Solution**	**Responsibility**	**Due Date**
Overproduction of sub-assembly 9	Reduce lot size to 50 pieces	John	12-16-04
Excess Conveyance from material rack to cell	Move material rack closer to cell	Mary	12-13-04
Excess Motion in tightening bolts	Replace ratchet wrench with pneumatic system	Steve	12-15-04
Production of defects and excess rework	Improve task lighting in cell	Ed	1-14-04
Excess travel to office to get copies	Purchase copy machine for cell	Hank	12-16-04
Excess Processing - too many burrs	Eliminate deburring operation: Improve reaming fixture	Ann	1-21-05
Excess Inventory of washers	Use smaller parts bins for washers	Ed	12-13-04
Excess Motion in selecting hand tools	Build shadow board	Ed	1-28-05
Waiting for tools	Establish tool Kanban control	Tom	1-28-05

229

CHAPTER 27

THE CELEBRATION

Friday morning was spent developing metrics and posting them in simple chart form on bulletin boards hung in the shearing, stamping, and assembly departments. Larry collected the latest data to compare to the original goals issued on Monday.

Original Goal	Actually Achieved By Friday
Stamping Improvement Team:	
Reduce setup time from 90 to 30 Minutes	28 Minutes
Reduce WIP by 90%	WIP at one machine reduced 90%
Install a "Pull" type material delivery system	Supermarket installed in stamping department
Assembly Improvement Team:	
Increase pieces per person per day by 25%	30% increase on one line so far
Reduce floor space by 25%	50% reduction on one line
Install a "Pull" type material delivery stystem	Supermarket installed in assembly department

Bob congratulated Larry for the achievements. "Larry, I am enormously proud of what was accomplished here this week. I am looking forward to your presentation at 1:00 this afternoon. It should be a stirring event. Let's have a look at your outline."

♦ A list of the daunting goals Brady gave to the team at the start of the week

♦ A team photograph

♦ Pictures of the team in action showing such activities as the Red Tag Campaign and data gathering.

♦ Before-during-after pictures of the layout

♦ Data summaries

♦ Performance against the goals.

♦ Future tasks for continuous improvement

Jim Brady had pretty much stayed in his office during the Kaizen week. That was his normal mode anyway—staying in his office and avoiding trips out to the factory. At 1:00 PM as scheduled, the Kaizen team made the presentation. Following the review of the data in the conference room, the team conducted a tour of the areas they have improved.

After the presentation and tour, Brady made a little speech. He said he was "blown away" by what had been accomplished in such a short period. He congratulated the team and issued impressive certificates of achievement that Larry Smith had prepared.

Larry had arranged for coffee and cake to be brought in after the discussions were over. After mingling with the shop personnel, Brady walked over to where Larry Smith was standing and shook his hand heartily. "Larry, I don't know how to thank you for what you've done here this week. You've opened my eyes to things that have to change and that change has to start with me. I've avoided the factory and never got to fully understand the processes or to get to know the people. I've been too tough on you. One thing is for sure— I'm not going to use those consultants. I think you have things in control as far as I'm concerned."

CHAPTER 28

LESSONS LEARNED

Sonic went on to conduct many more Kaizen events throughout their facility. All Lean and Kaizen activities were led by Larry Smith, who, in addition to his job of running operations, had become the company's Lean Promotions Officer. Jim Brady became a new man. He no longer had charts on his office wall and instead spent a great deal of time in the factory meeting with people, encouraging them, and reading the charts they were maintaining in their respective areas.

Let's leave the world of Larry Smith, Bob Simms, and Jim Brady. They will do fine. Here's a list of the benefits they will enjoy by implementing Lean techniques:

√ Reduced customer lead time

√ Reduced rejects and rework

√ Reduced floor space

√ Wide participation in improvement activities by employees

√ Improved cash flow

√ Reduced overtime

√ Increased profits

Implementing Lean is a tough challenge. Not too many companies in the U.S. have achieved it. Those that have enjoy better cost, quality, and delivery performance because they have learned how to achieve more and more by using fewer resources.

The following table lists metrics used to describe the performance of companies that have achieved Lean status.

Performance of Factories with Broad Plant wide Lean Intitiatives (Based upon Industry Week magazine's Census of Manufacturers)	
Metrics	
Finished product first pass yield	99%
Scrap and rework costs as a percentage of sales	<1%
Warranty costs as a percentage of sales	<.5%
Five Year manufacturing cycle time reduction	>20%
Customer Lead time	<5 days
On-time delivery rate	>98%
Annual raw materials inventory turns	12 turns
Annual work in progress inventory turns	16.5 turns
Annual finished goods inventory turns	12.6 turns
Total annual inventory turns	9 turns
Productivity as dollar value of annual shipments per employee	$200,000

Although this story has been fictionalized, theirs is not atypical of the experience of the courageous companies that embarked on a Lean journey. There are some important lessons to be learned from the experience of the people at Sonic:

<u>Executive Leadership</u>. The chief executive of the firm to be improved must be a wholeheartedly enthusiastic supporter of the conversion to Lean. He or she must be willing to issue a "call to action" and make it clear that the company cannot continue in their present operating method.

<u>Project Management</u>. The project manager responsible for the company's conversion to Lean must be a "fanatic" and perhaps see this as a career opportunity.

<u>Success Planning</u>. You can't just "dive into" the Lean conversion. A comprehensive success plan must first be developed. This plan needs a realistic timetable, specific levels of expectations and a clear delineation of who will be responsible for what, and when.

<u>Training</u>. Education is vital. Investment must be made in training people at every level of the organization. The shop floor personnel must be engaged in the Lean conversion (not victims of it).

<u>Pilot Project Success</u>. Every journey begins with a single step. But great care must be given in selecting the first step in the Lean conversion. If the first step is to be a Kaizen event, pick a project that will be a winner.

<u>Consultants</u>. It's wise to hire a consultant or *sensei* for two reasons. First, an experienced consultant has been through many Lean implementations before and, therefore, owns a "template" to support a smooth implementation. And second, most manufacturing managers become "factory blind." That is, the waste that they walk past every day now looks *normal*. It won't look normal to an outsider.

<u>Follow Through</u>. Tennis experts say that the follow through of the stroke has more to do with the ball hitting the target than does the stroke approach. Similarly, the follow-through on each element of the Lean conversion is vital in sustaining and propagating whatever initial gains are made.

> *When you can measure what you are speaking about, and express it in numbers, you know something about it; but when you cannot measure it, when you cannot express it in numbers, your knowledge is of a meager and unsatisfactory kind: it may be the beginning of knowledge, but you have scarcely in your thoughts advanced to the stage of science.*
>
> Lord Kelvin

APPENDIX A

JUST IN TIME (JIT) 100 Points

	LEVEL 1		LEVEL 2		LEVEL 3		Score
	Description	Score	Description	Score	Description	Score	
A. Layout	Process oriented.	(0-3)	Mixed Layout Process & Product Orientation. Some cells.	(4-7)	Product oriented layout with integrated cells and multiple machines per operator.	(8-10)	
B. Scheduling	Poor scheduling leading to frequent stock outs & constant replenishing.	(0-6)	Relatively stable master production schedule with limited expediting.	(7-14)	Manufacturing schedule directly coupled with market demand.	(15-20)	
C. Maintenance	On-demand maintenance with frequent breakdowns.	(0-3)	Established preventative maintenance with infrequent breakdowns.	(4-7)	Total preventative maintenance. With specific standardized maintenance task for the operators.	(8-10)	
D. Inventory Turns	Less than 10 turns per year.	(0-6)	Higher inventory turns 10-25 per year.	(7-14)	High inventory turns approaching 25 per year.	(15-20)	
E. Lead Times	Long lead times. Over 4 times factory throughput time.	(0-6)	Relatively short lead times for selected products. Less than 4 times factory throughput.	(7-14)	Extremely low lead times. Less than 2 times factory throughput time.	(15-20)	
F. Metrics	Labor efficiency & machine utilization.	(0-3)	Schedule compliance, labor efficiency & machine utilization.	(4-7)	Lead time, quality level, & value-added ratio.	(8-10)	
G. Changeover	Lengthy changeovers.	(0-3)	Quick changeover (minutes) in some operations.	(4-7)	Changeovers measured in minutes for the whole operation.	(8-10)	

QUALITY ACHIEVEMENT 100 Points							
	LEVEL 1		LEVEL 2		LEVEL 3		
	Description	Score	Description	Score	Description	Score	Score
A. Process Capability	Machines & Processes unable to hold tolerances. Cpk < 1.00 or processes unstable.	(0-6)	Good machine & Process Capability with SPC/SQC on limited basis. Cpk ~ 1.33	(7-14)	Machines & Process continually improved using SPC/SQC tools. Cpk > 1.67	(15-20)	
B. Quality Assurance	Large powerful inspection department.	(0-3)	Strong QA department with analytical capability charged with quality responsibility.	(4-7)	Highly trained workforce responsible for quality & continuous improvement.	(8-10)	
C. Scrap & Rework	Large rates of scrap & rework.	(0-3)	High rates of scrap & rework, but visual efforts in reduction.	(4-7)	Very low rates of scrap & rework measured in parts per million.	(8-10)	
D. Workmanship	Low skills training.	(0-3)	Good skills and training.	(4-7)	Highly skilled and trained versatile workforce.	(8-10)	
E. Measurement	Operators measured on quantity.	(0-3)	Operators measured on quality & quantity.	(4-7)	Operators measured on improvements, quality, & quantity.	(8-10)	
F. External Failure	Large volume of customer returns & high warranty costs.	(0-3)	Low customer returns but warranty still a problem & handled by Quality Dept.	(4-7)	Non-existent customer returns, very low warranty costs. Mistake proof devices.	(8-10)	
G. Supplier Quality	Large number of vendors, 100% inspection of received goods.	(0-6)	Fewer vendors with source inspection & quality audits of incoming goods	(7-14)	Level of customer satisfaction is quantified and targets for improvement are established.	(15-20)	
H. Customer Satisfaction	There is no formal method to record customer complaints or act upon them.	(0-6)	Customer complaints are recorded and acted upon.	(7-14)	Level of customer satisfaction is quantified and targets for improvement are established.	(15-20)	

243

PRODUCTION METHODS 100 Points

	LEVEL 1		LEVEL 2		LEVEL 3		Score
	Description	Score	Description	Score	Description	Score	
A. Work Flow	Work done in batches to amortize setups. Flow of the product is difficult to understand. There is no sense of order.	(0-6)	One-piece flow demonstrated in some operations. Flow follows a logic but is not synchronous.	(7-14)	One-piece flow demonstrated in majority of operations. Factory is arranged to give synchronous flow without batches between operations.	(15-20)	
B. Inventory	Buffer inventory used to assure smooth flow.	(0-6)	Stock replenished by standard batch sizes.	(7-14)	Stock replenished by smallest practical lot sizes.	(15-20)	
C. Rework	Rework performed in same area as standard production.	(0-3)	Rework separated from standard production.	(4-7)	Rework separated from standard production, and designated as a Quality Cost.	(8-10)	
D. Process Status	Process status very difficult to ascertain.	(0-3)	Process status is identified but is not immediately clear.	(4-7)	Process status is clearly visible.	(8-10)	

(Continued on Next Page)

244

PRODUCTION METHODS (Continued)

	LEVEL 1		LEVEL 2		LEVEL 3		Score
	Description	Score	Description	Score	Description	Score	
E. Cell Technology	No application of cell technology.	(0-6)	Cell technology applied in some operations with plans for expansion.	(7-14)	Extensive use of synchronously linked autonomous manufacturing cell technology.	(15-20)	
F. Automation	No automation present, or automation is inappropriate and extravagant.	(0-6)	Adequate automation is evident in some areas but lacks flexibility.	(7-14)	Automation is used to ensure consistency & eliminate hazards. Loading, unloading & defect segregation are mechanized. Automated processes are highly flexible.	(15-20)	

FACILITY 50 Points	LEVEL 1		LEVEL 2		LEVEL 3		Score
	Description	Score	Description	Score	Description	Score	**Score**
A. House Keeping	Facility gives the impression of being sloppy and dirty.	(0-6)	Some areas are maintained to a good degree of order and cleanliness.	(7-14)	Facility gives the impression of a high degree of cleanliness and "a place for everything & everything in its place."	(15-20)	
B. Traffic	Aisles are not clearly marked and are cluttered.	(0-3)	Aisles are clearly marked but materials are stored within designated aisles.	(4-7)	Aisles are clearly marked, clear & clean.	(8-10)	
C. Storage	Material is stored in unmarked containers, or just on the floor.	(0-3)	Most material is stored in containers & in designated areas.	(4-7)	No parts are stored in unmarked containers. All material that is not in use is cleared form the production area.	(8-10)	
D. Condition	Walls and floors are old and faded or dirty. Poor levels of lighting. Poor safety features.	(0-3)	Walls & floors are old and faded or dirty. Good levels of lighting and safety features.	(4-7)	Fresh, bright paint on walls. Floors in good condition. Very good light levels & safety features.	(8-10)	

STANDARDS 50 Points

	LEVEL 1		LEVEL 2		LEVEL 3		Score
	Description	Score	Description	Score	Description	Score	
A. Process	Most process are human dependent. Different operators perform the same task differently.	(0-6)	Some operations have been standardized.	(7-14)	Very few processes are human dependent because critical processes are automated or highly standardized.	(15-20)	
B. Work Instructions	No written work instructions are provided.	(0-6)	Some written work instructions are provided and are fromally controlled.	(7-14)	Written work instructions are provided, formally controlled, are living documents and constantly improved and updated.	(15-20)	
C. Information	There are no posted metrics, understanding of the performance goals is very limited.	(0-3)	Goals and performance against them are posted in some areas, or are available for interested people to see.	(4-7)	All critical metrics are conspicuously posted so everyone knows how well they are performing.	(8-10)	

PERSONNEL MANAGEMENT 100 Points

	LEVEL 1		LEVEL 2		LEVEL 3		Score
	Description	Score	Description	Score	Description	Score	
A. Labor Relations	Adversarial labor-management relations.	(0-6)	Stable labor-management relations.	(7-14)	Labor management relations based upon trust and continuous two-way communications.	(15-20)	
B. Organization	Rigid or complicated organizational structure, more than 6 management layers, more than 10 job classifications.	(0-3)	Simple organizational structure, lines of authority & responsibility are clear. Some examples of organization with few layers.	(4-7)	Simple organizational structure, less than 5 management layers, less than 5 job classifications.	(8-10)	
C. Leadership	No one understands management vision. There is no comprehension of short term improvement goals.	(0-6)	Management vision is not uniformly interpreted. Mile stones for improvement are established for the upcoming month and change constantly.	(7-14)	Management vision is clear to everyone. There are qualitative expectations of improvement goals by management which define the critical success factors for the next 90 days.	(15-20)	
D. Work Practice	Restrictive authoritarian work practice.	(0-3)	Some flexible work practice.	(4-7)	Very flexible work practice, actively encourage cross training.	(8-10)	

(Continued on Next Page)

PERSONNEL MANAGEMENT 100 Points (CONTINUED)

	LEVEL 1		LEVEL 2		LEVEL 3		Score
	Description	Score	Description	Score	Description	Score	
E. Motivation	Low motivation & morale, high turnover. High aversion to risk taking.	(0-6)	Motivated with good moral, stable workforce. Some degree of employee involvement.	(7-14)	Highly motivated team environment, high degree of perceived employee ownership and contribution. Hourly workforce actively involved in problem solving & process improvement.	(15-20)	
F. Development	No management development.	(0-6)	Personnel department involved with management development.	(7-14)	Personnel department facilitates development & involvement in all aspects of the business. Encourages cross-corporation promotion.	(15-20)	

Score Summary
Maximum Score — 500   Company:
                         Date:

JIT	
Quality Achievement	
Production Methods	
Facility	
Standards	
Personnel Management	
GRAND TOTAL	

INDEX

S

T

V

Value Stream 8
Value Stream Map 8, 51, 101
  Current State 126
    Example Of 128, 129
  Future State 126
    Example Of 129
Velocity 59, 75, 120
Visual Workplace 141

W

Waste 7 *See also* MUDA
Waste Elimination 138
'Why' List 193
'Why' Questions 180
Work-In-Process (WIP) 163

Y

Yellow Tag Campaign 202
Yellow Tags 201
Yin and Yang 61

ABOUT THE AUTHOR

JERRY FEINGOLD is a highly sought after management consultant in the field of Lean manufacturing. He conducts work in the United States and Europe with a wide variety of manufacturing companies including consumer, commercial, and medical product producers, food processors, and government contractors.

He began independent consulting in 1998 after retiring from industry where he worked for thirty-four years in senior executive positions at four Fortune 100 companies. He started Continuous Improvement Consultancy in Ventura, California helping companies improve their operations through the elimination of waste in the factory as well as service and administrative areas.

Originally an industrial engineer (he holds a BS in Industrial Engineering and an MBA), Jerry rose to the executive level where he conducted numerous successful domestic and international start-ups and turnarounds. While employed in industry he became an enthusiastic practitioner of Kaizen and other Japanese Lean management techniques that he studied in Japan and applied there. In addition to numerous speaking engagements at colleges and universities, Jerry has been featured on public television and talk radio.

Getting Lean is the result of Jerry's many years of experience helping companies become more competitive.